T O P E E L A N
ONION

TO PEEL AN
ONION

THE LIVES OF GERDA ROZE, A MEMOIR

GERDA ROZE

Library of Congress Control Number:		2012919361
ISBN:	Hardcover	978-1-4797-3428-3
	Softcover	978-1-4797-3427-6
	Ebook	978-1-4797-3429-0

This book was printed in the United States of America.

To order additional copies of this book, contact:
Xlibris Corporation
1-888-795-4274
www.Xlibris.com
Orders@Xlibris.com
114816

CONTENTS

For Peter

All that follows, Peter, will be written for you.
Whether this turns into a best-selling book or
forever remains a rough draft of my memoirs, may
it reveal something to you about the life of a woman
who happened to be your grandmother.

ACKNOWLEDGMENTS

Now that my memoir is about ready to go to production, there is one more detail to be taken care of—the acknowledgment of those who in some way helped me enrich and complete my project. They had ideas, suggestions, and good advice. Most helpful were those who asked me questions, leading me to remember and think about incidents from the past and, ultimately, to write them down.

The first two who come to mind—who did exactly that—were my daughter-in-law Koren Rhoads in Florida and my cousin Sibilla Pālena, MD, in Riga. I have known Koren over thirty-five years now, and she certainly knows my life in detail. Her memory is better than mine these days, and she sometimes had to remind me of stories I had told her over the years. "Don't forget to include this one in your book," she would say. Thank you, Koren.

Cousin Sibilla, on the other hand, kept reminding me of events I described to her during our ten-year correspondence period prior to my second return trip to Latvia when she and I were finally able to visit. What's more, she was able to fill in missing links about my paternal grandparents and support these stories with old family portraits.

Yes, family photos are always a great catalyst for reliving and reconstructing the past. When my mother and I fled Riga, I ripped out a few photos from our family albums, which were important to me in that moment. I carried those in my handbag. There are few living witnesses from my generation still around, so I relied upon my memory and wrote truthfully about my personal experiences and stories related to me over the years by sources I considered reliable.

I would also like to thank art curator Bruce Kozma, Dr. Michael Preston, John Sasko, and Bill Waitzman, who took time from their busy schedules to read my early draft and give me helpful suggestions.

And of course, it's the editor who puts the crowning touch on a manuscript. I was very fortunate to work with Pat Kozma, owner of Manhattan Manuscripts, whose competence and professionalism greatly contributed to the final completion of the book. Thank you, Pat, for the many hours spent on my memoir. You were the first reader to whom I poured out my heart about my long and complicated life story.

UNFOLDING THE STORY

It has been a while—actually, a very long while—since I prepared myself to sit down and write about my own life. I think of it now and then though I don't often actually do it. It isn't that I want to create a literary treasure. It's more a matter of sharing my experience with my grandson Peter and maybe his future children. I imagine him reading of his Grandma Gerda and thinking about her life—how the strange, curious, wonderful, awful threads of Grandmother Gerda's experience intertwine with his own.

That was my original intention. But now that I finally begin to scratch the surface of a life long gone, I run into roadblocks I hadn't expected. It sometimes is painful to dig up the past. Good memories are also surprisingly hard to relive. Even at this moment, I am so emotionally involved with my past that it brings out tears, and I am only at the very beginning.

One memory brings out others—all somewhat connected, yet also somehow disjointed. Sometimes it feels like a big mumbo jumbo. Time runs short. So at this moment, my task is to put down on paper as much as I can and hope to rewrite it later. Maybe I am beginning to understand writers who say once you get into serious writing, it drives you to continue and makes it impossible to stop.

I

Heritage

The Day of My Birth

I was born in Riga, Latvia, on February 4, 1925. On the map, Latvia is located in the northeast corner of Europe where the winters are cold and long, and it's not unusual to be buried under snow on Easter morning. But on that particular first week in February, unusually warm winds crossed the Baltic shores. The sun shone warmly, and the snow began to melt.

My mother and her newborn baby girl were brought home from the hospital in Uncle Rozīt's open Opel sports car. I can't picture that now, but that's how it was told to me later by other family members, raising their eyebrows: "After all, February was still the middle of winter in Latvia." My mother was twenty-nine, and my father was two years older. He called my mother Ernotchka, a loving Russian nickname for Erna. After six years of marriage, the arrival of their daughter was an exhilarating event, made more so, I imagine, by the new sports car. Of course, I was too young then to enjoy either the ride or my arrival as much as my parents did.

It was customary for immediate families and very close friends to celebrate the arrival of a newborn. In the early afternoon, the dining room table was set to serve tea, coffee, or a glass of wine, together with an assortment of home-baked sweets. In the center of the table was a large cake in the shape of a two-foot-long pretzel. This cake, called kliņģeris, was our cake for all festivities—birthdays, name days, and important holidays. The kliņģeris was made from a yeast dough that traditionally contained flour, butter, milk, raisins, citron, Spanish saffron, and roasted almonds. It was decorated with whole almonds, and just before it went into the oven, it was brushed with a couple of raw eggs to achieve a shiny light brown surface during the baking.

Being chosen to bake the kliņģeris for such an occasion—especially so the arrival of a newborn—was considered to be a distinct honor. When the day came for this particular kliņģeris, it turned out there were two candidates for the honorable job. One was my maternal grandmother Elizabeth; the other

1

was my father's Aunt Marija, sister of my departed Grandmother Matilda. Each of them was certain it was she who was chosen to do the honors. Oh, my!

Soon, it wasn't just Elizabeth and Marija who were battling it out, but the two families joined into the argument too. As it turned out, Grandmother Elizabeth baked the kliņģeris. But meanwhile, my mother, still in her hospital bed, became so upset with the uproar she came down with "milk fever" and had to engage a wet nurse for me. The entire incident was unnecessary and unfortunate, but it left a permanent rift in the relationship between the two families, which we all endured in our various ways.

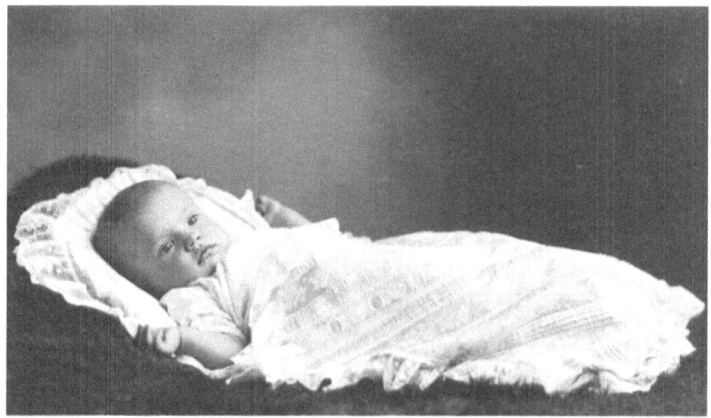

The Day of my Baptism
Riga, April 13, 1925

What Came before Gerda

But my beginning is flavored by ancestry too. So let's go back at least a century to help the reader better understand the geography and the times in the history of my ancestors before World War I.

Russia's vast borders stretched from the Ural Mountains on the European side to the Baltic Sea on the West and consisted of many smaller nations. Originally, Russia proper was a rather small area around Moscow. All the other countries were later conquered or simply occupied. Through the broad strokes of history, some of these countries became independent after WWI, as did Latvia on November 18, 1918. Others became satellites of the Soviet Union. Riga was at the crossroads where two cultures met—Russian and German. The official government language was Russian while individual nationals spoke their own languages. Beginning in the twelfth and thirteenth centuries, German culture began to invade the Western border areas of Russia, when Germans began to settle in the Baltics. Long before my time, the street names of Riga were displayed in three languages: Russian, German, and Latvian. Beyond the city, the countryside was all Latvian. As in my mother's family, it was not unusual for a family to send their boys to Russian gymnasiums while their daughters attended German finishing schools.

My Paternal Grandparents

My paternal grandfather, Alexander Semënowitch Podostrojecs, was born in Riga in 1865 of Russian parents. As a young man, he aimed to become a priest and attended a Russian Orthodox Seminary for two years. Ultimately, he changed his mind and chose a career in law enforcement. Before the turn of the century, he served the czar as secretary to the governor of the Courland province, residing in Jēkabpils. There, Alexander gradually advanced to the position of police commissioner, with a military rank of colonel in the czar's army.

Alexander Semënowitch Podostrojecs
My Paternal Grandfather
1865-1930

Matilda Podostrojecs, nee Jansons
My Paternal Grandmother
1865-1922

My father's mother, Matilda Jansons, was both Latvian and Lutheran. She and my grandfather had two sons—Kolja (Nikolai) and Vladimir—and four daughters—Sacha (Alexandra), Sonja (Sophia), Olja (Olga), and Lisa (Elizabeth). My father, Kolja, was their third child, born in Jēkabpils in 1894. His early childhood was spent between two homes. One was his father's official residence in Jēkabpils, and the other was their country estate in Grodno.

My father and his younger brother Vladimir enjoyed the open-space country living where, early on in their lives, they were exposed to game hunting. On the estate in Grodno, game hunting was Grandpa Alexander's favorite way to pass time with his guests. Grandma Matilda related to my mother that at one time they owned twenty-three hunting dogs!

One day, according to Grandma Matilda, she was doing her shopping in town where she ran into their parish priest. "How is Kolja doing?" he asked. "Is he getting better?"

Grandma Matilda knew her son had not been ill as the priest had presumed but was enjoying himself in the woods where he preferred to spend his time hunting. She recovered a bit from her embarrassment that Kolja had been truant from school and discovered that, indeed, he had missed quite a lot more than she thought.

Game hunting remained for my father a lifetime passion—one that knew no limits. My mother often referred to it as his "obsession."

Soon after the revolution broke out in 1917, my grandfather was arrested by the Bolsheviks and sentenced to die by shooting in the Central Prison in Riga. His crime was being a police commissioner, having served the czar years before. His best friend—an orthodox priest he had known since they were children—was found guilty of being an enemy of the people, solely because of his religious affiliation.

The prison where they both were confined was overcrowded with political prisoners. Periodically, the Bolshevik guards would come in, call out names of several prisoners, and order them into the courtyard. There, these prisoners were executed.

One day, in the corner of a large cell, my grandfather and the priest sat on the dirt floor, waiting to hear their names called. The room slowly emptied and the last group was called. Incredulously, the two of them had been spared. Was this an oversight on the part of the guards? Had their names been omitted from the list of prisoners scheduled for execution that day? We'll never know. But several days later, the Bolsheviks retreated from Riga, and Grandpa Alexander and his friend walked out of prison.

Following the Russian Revolution in 1917, my grandparents lost all their property when Grodno became part of Byelorussia. So they returned to Latvia on the Baltic seashore near Riga where they owned a small villa in Majori. Here, they would live for the rest of their lives.

My Maternal Grandparents

My maternal grandmother, Elizabeth, was raised by her widowed mother Katrīna Indrik who worked hard to provide every possible advantage for her only daughter, including the finest finishing schools. My grandmother attended school for nine years and spoke fluent French and German.

My maternal grandfather, Julius Rozīt (or as we called him, *Opapa*), was a guild's master blacksmith, taking after his father Kaspars Rozīt, a master carpenter. All his life, Opapa worked as a designer blacksmith for the Russian Transcontinental Locomotive Company in Riga. There, he worked building railroad cars for the vast Russian railroad system, including the Trans-Siberian railroad.

The custom in those days was for apprentices to be trained by a Master, and occasionally some of these young men lived as boarders in my grandparents' home.

Grandpa Julius was born in Mitau and came from a solid background of craftspeople. He became an active member of the Latvian Trade Union known as Latviešu Arodbiedrība. Opapa was also an active member and leader in the prestigious Riga's Latvian Association (Rīgas Latviešu Biedrība), also known as Our Latvian Mother (Māmuļa).

My Maternal Grandparents
Julius Rozit and Elizabeth Rozit, nee Indrik

I recall one special event when I was, maybe, ten. I was visiting my grandparents along with my two cousins—nine-year-old Zigismunds and five-year-old Edgars. Omama must have been in one of her rare good moods because she told us of Opapa's leadership position in "Māmuļa." In their annual parades, Opapa could be seen marching at the head and wearing a top hat. To make it more dramatic for us children, Omama brought out an old, dusty hatbox from her bedroom closet, which contained Grandpa's hat.

For the times, Opapa made a lot of money and provided an affluent lifestyle for his family. Omama, for her part, was never satisfied with Opapa's earnings, which she spent as fast as he made it. They had four children. The two boys were Arvīds and Artūrs, and the two girls were my mother Erna and her sister Elza.

Grandma was used to the better things of life. Omama had been employed when she was a young woman as a governess and fine seamstress in the German nobility court in Mitau. This would become the main seat of German aristocracy in the Baltics, and soon after the First World War, Mitau was renamed Jelgava. Jelgava's Pils, the castle where my grandmother worked before the turn of the century, still exists—the remains of a glorious past. But there in the Castle, Grandma Elizabeth became accustomed to luxury. I wonder sometimes how it is she came to marry a blacksmith.

She loved to read, and her home was stocked with hundreds of books. In my recollection, they were all bound in red leather, and I think they were probably novels. I'll bet she spent a lot of time neglecting her children in favor of finishing yet another chapter in one of her books.

Grandma Elizabeth and Opapa never spoke to each other that I can recall, and they said very little to us grandchildren. On holidays, we made traditional visits to their home and occasionally at other times too. Opapa would touch the tip of my nose to acknowledge my presence without ever a word.

He was a very good-looking man—tall, with beautiful white hair. His beloved fox terrier Jimmy was always with him. The two of them lived for each other. But Jimmy was a horror. He'd nip and bite anyone other than Opapa whenever they least expected it. Even the mail carriers hated him, and Opapa had to bribe them and other delivery men with money and gifts. As for us children, we did whatever it took to stay out of Jimmy's way.

When Opapa was in his early eighties, he had a stroke and was rushed to the hospital. For three days, Jimmy did not leave Grandpa's empty bed, and that's where Jimmy died. There are Latvian stories of mythological dogs so loyal that they grieve for days at the graves of their masters, then die of their own broken hearts. I'm certain that's what happened to Jimmy.

II

Journey through Europe

My Family

My Earliest Memory

My own earliest memories are of Olaine—maybe 1929, early spring. I was a tot of four when my mother underwent major surgery, and I went to stay with her sister Elza. I had a problem pronouncing the *z*, so I called her Tante Ella. For the first time in my life, I was away from Mami, and this was a very trying time for me. I recall the tears shed as I cried myself to sleep every night. Tante Ella would try to console me with fairy tales she made up.

Tante Ella was two years older than my mother, and she was a very warm person who never took life too seriously. I remember how nice it was to sit in her lap where she would hug me and kiss me. I loved her dearly!

At last, Mami came home from the hospital, and I was allowed to return shortly thereafter. Finally! But I had to promise not to ask Mami to lift me and not to touch her tummy because that's where it hurt. Even so, coming home from Tante Ella's was the happiest moment of my young life.

Our summers were spent away from the city as was the custom in those days. We occasionally went to the seashore, but more often, we went to the countryside. Where to spend our vacation was always up to my father. His decision was based on the time and place where game-hunting season would provide him with his own pastime.

This often dictated a "summer vacation" in early spring or late fall. When my mother's friends asked about her summer vacation, my mother would tell them, "We always seem to be travelling in the opposite direction from normal vacationers. In fall, when they are returning to the city, that's when we're leaving it."

This particular year, my parents rented a summerhouse in the country in a little town called Olaine. It was early spring, with spotty snow still on the ground. Our baggage was sent ahead to our destination. Mother and I took the train.

We were the only passengers who got off the train in Olaine. Curiously, no one was at the station to meet us when we arrived. Of course, I was too little to question my mother or ask what we were going to do now. A shrill whistle announced the train's departure, and the two of us were left standing alone on the platform. The place was deserted. Mother decided immediately that we'd walk the mile and a half to the village.

Today, as I think of it, I try to put myself in her place: standing there with a four-year-old child, herself still recovering from major surgery. What options did she have? For whatever inexcusable reason we found ourselves in this predicament, I'm certain my mother thought only of her child and her responsibility to get us to our destination. As for me, nothing mattered in my world nearly as much as that I was together with my mami again.

It was a cool day, and my mother wore her fur coat. I was bundled in wool overalls, fur coat and cap, and high rubber boots. We had walked quite a distance through a forest smattered with patches of snow. The air was cool and clear. I struggled with my bulky attire as Mami tried to encourage me. "It's not that far anymore, Gerdiņa," she said more than once. "Just around the corner."

As we marched on, step after step, my boots got heavier and heavier until I could barely lift my legs. Finally, I said, "Mami, I know you are not allowed to carry me because of your sick tummy, but please let me rest for a while here on this tree stump. I'm very tired."

After I rested, we continued our walk through the forest. Soon, we came to a fallen tree blocking our way, probably the consequence of a winter blizzard. Mami took my hand, and we arduously circumvented the roadblock on our troublesome journey. As she would relate to me much later, from the moment we struggled with that downed tree, all my attention was directed toward understanding why our journey was blocked. "You kept asking again and again why anyone would make our journey so hard to travel."

Now an old woman myself, I often still wonder the very same thing.

My Parents

My father was a police officer. My mother, a pharmacist by profession, became a housewife after I was born. In character and temperament, they could not have been more different from each other. In part, I imagine their upbringing accounted for some of that difference.

My mother was born and grew up in Riga, a metropolitan city and the last West European culture centre of the Russian Empire, sometimes called the Little Paris. My father, on the other hand, was born in Jēkabpils, a small town near the Russian border. Jēkabpils was the governor's seat for the Courland Province in the Czar Empire. He and his brother and sisters were brought up primarily by nannies and tutors. In Old Russia, it was the father's religion that determined that of his offspring. So my father and his siblings were all Russian Orthodox.

Nikolajs Roze
My Father
1894-1977

Erna Roze, nee Rozit
My Mother
1896-1971

Oddly, the difference between my mother's Lutheranism and my father's religion was never a particular obstacle for them. Of course, the rules of Old Russia no longer applied in the 1925 democratic government system into which I was born, and my mother ensured that I was baptized Lutheran when I came into the world. In my parents' home, Russian Easter was celebrated, as was Christmas. On Christmas Eve, in fact, we all attended a Lutheran service—my mother, my father, and I.

I don't know what religion meant to my father, if anything. I asked him sometimes why he never attended his own church or went to confession. What he told me was this: "I would not be able to tell the truth to the priest, and I would not lie to him either. That's why I don't go to confession."

My father was not an intellectual by nature, but he loved to read the Russian classics. His favorite writer was Turgenev, known for his hunting stories.

We were not wealthy, by any stretch. My father, after all, was only a police officer. But my mother did wonders with his earnings. She created a beautiful home for us, often going overboard with purchases I'm sure we could barely afford. When I was six, my parents bought me a concert piano at a price that far exceeded my father's annual income. Still, somehow, in the end, she managed. Her talent and ingenuity were always in evidence.

In my home, my mother was the disciplinarian. I never remember my father angry with me, nor, God forbid, punishing me. It was always my mother who "straightened me out." It was also she who made important decisions. My father likely recognized early on in their marriage that she was the leader. I'd often hear him say, "Just do what you think is best, Ernotchka."

And Then There Was Arthur

Let me tell you about Arthur—Arturs Berglunds—who came into my life when I was four. He was married to my mother's best girlfriend Elza Brambe, nicknamed Effie. After the revolution, Effie and her family—evacuees from Riga—temporarily settled in Moscow. Arthur was a student at the Moscow Politechnicum, studying electro-engineering. Both of them were born and grew up in Riga. Arthur and Effie's only child, a little girl, died in infancy; and they returned to Latvia with thousands of other Latvian refugees in the early 1920s.

Eventually, Arthur and Effie began to go their separate ways, and one day Effie told him to leave. Of course, he didn't much like the idea of leaving his comfortable home and simply refused to go anywhere. So one Saturday morning, Effie called my parents and asked them to come pick him up and take him into their home "until he could find his own place and settle down."

I remember distinctly the morning Arthur moved in with us. I stood in my crib holding on to the rail, still dressed in my long nightgown. I watched Arthur walk into the room with my parents. My mother would later tell me this story. "You were always a very serious child. When we brought Arthur into the room, you looked surprised and opened your eyes wide and demanded to know who this gentleman was." It was customary in those days for a young person to address an older relative or friend of the family as uncle or "tante." So he became Uncle Arthur to me.

Our home was quite adequate, and Arthur had his own room where he could live the life of a bachelor. Years later, Tante Effie decided to legalize their separation and file for divorce. When the judge announced their divorce, Uncle Arthur presented Effie with a beautiful bouquet of red roses. I never heard either of them speak ill of the other, and I imagined that must be what is meant by an amicable divorce.

And then there was Arthur
1891-1977

Uncle Arthur was always very good to me. He would take me places and tell me stories—mostly stories that reflected his travels. I imagined then that he covered a lot of geography when he would disappear and then return when I least expected it—something that happened frequently during his stay with us then. Later, throughout his lifetime, that pattern continued, and Arthur always seemed to be there for us with his kind and generous nature.

Early Education and Music Studies

I began piano lessons when I was six. I hated practicing. But my mother was determined and would not relent to my crying and practicing, practicing and crying. One evening I sat at the piano and practiced and cried and cried and practiced. My father in the next room lost patience, or maybe he just could not tolerate my heartbreaking cries. He walked into the room where my mother worked on her embroidery, sitting next to me, watching and counting while I practiced and cried.

"Why don't you leave the kid alone?" my father said. "Don't you see how unhappy she is?"

Still, my mother persevered. In time, I learned to love both music and my piano. By the time I was in high school, I was studying under the well-known Czech-born concert pianist and pedagogue, Professor Ludmila Goman Dombrovska at the Latvian State Conservatory (Latvijas Valsts Konservātorija). I had become an accomplished pianist. Professor Goman sponsored my scholarship when our financial situation became dire following the 1940 Russian occupation of Latvia. So I continued my studies for free.

Professor Goman told my mother I had earned the grant through hard work and not through any special talent. It was Professor Goman's belief that one with talent often does not achieve what hard work alone can accomplish. In time, I came to realize she was right. I was not musically gifted, and all my accomplishments were due purely to hard work—practice and tears, as I think of it now.

At age 8, I dreamed of becoming an actress

Obviously, I was meant to be a boy, so I had to accompany Dad on his hunting trips (1933)

But I did learn to love my music! There were days I practiced for hours and hours. As a music student, I was expected to be deeply involved in the music world. I was required to attend a concert, recital, or opera at least once a week. Of course, I had long since begun to visit our National Opera. My debut visit was when I was twelve.

To celebrate the occasion, my parents gave me a black silk evening bag with a tiny sterling silver change purse, a little notepad with a silver pencil, and my own mother-of-pearl opera glasses. I even recall the short navy blue silk dress I wore that night, with a pinned-on yellow rose.

By the time I was sixteen, I was working hard at music while pursuing my academic program at a "classic gymnasium." I had been admitted to the Riga First State Gymnasium (Rīgas I. Valsts Ģimnāzija) for a seven-year program at the age of twelve in 1937 following stiff entrance exams. At that time in Latvia, every child was required to have an eight-year education—two years of preschool, then six of elementary. Further schooling was optional and tuition had to be paid.

My school had a strict academic curriculum. We were taught Latin, Greek, and two modern languages—French and German—besides Latvian, of course. A very high percentage of our graduates went on to universities, most often choosing medicine or law.

I graduated and received my diploma in 1944.

The War Begins

Soviet Army Occupies Latvia

In 1939, the war between Germany and England was declared, and the Soviet Union needed to build their defense installations along the coast of the Baltic Sea in anticipation of a possible German attack. In order to do this, they needed an exit to the sea, which led them to occupy the three Baltic countries of Lithuania, Latvia, and Estonia.

In June of 1940, Russian troops crossed our borders and occupied Latvia. The official communiqué from our Latvian President Kārlis Ulmanis was that "our neighbor, the Soviet Union, has come in as a friend to protect us from the enemy," meaning Germany. "I urge you to stay where you are and remain calm, while I'll remain in my place . . ." After an overnight occupation, the Russians remained a year and thirteen days, during which time they brought terror and destruction to our peaceful country.

What could we do? The three Baltic states altogether had a population of about five and a half million compared to 170 million from the Soviet Union. We were no match for the Soviet power. We were trapped.

The Russian troops who arrived were poorly equipped and attired. This was not the image of a superpower although endless gray lines of these soldiers and tanks passed through Latvia from east to west, headed for the Baltic Sea.

I don't know the reason—perhaps upon orders—but the Russian troops had no contact with the civilian population, which lent an air of surreality to the spectacle these invaders presented to us. Of course, that did not last long, and soon their voices could be heard all over the land.

The Russian soldiers were stunned by the wealth of choice presented in our stores. Food, clothing, and daily consumer goods were in abundance when they visited our main Market Halls in Riga, where customers were offered plenty of meat, butter, and everything else imaginable. Many stories—sometimes very funny ones—circulated about Russian soldiers' reactions in the marketplace we were accustomed to.

One day, a short Russian soldier stood next to me at the market. I watched him in silence a while—how his disbelieving eyes took in the sight of the spread in front of him. Finally, he decided to purchase something and asked the butcher, "How long will this exhibit last?" I giggled, but I didn't dare let him see me. Another day I was buying a pair of shoes for myself, and I overheard a soldier ask the saleslady if he could buy *two* pairs of beautiful leather boots—one for himself and one for a friend.

The Communist government established itself in Latvia by arresting our president and other high government officials. After his arrest, President Ulmanis was deported to Siberia where he subsequently died. Then, they called for a "free election" to let the people decide the system of government. But "free election" for the Soviet Union meant only that voters were "free" to affirm the single choice they were given, which resulted in a 98.99 percent vote for annexation to Big Brother Stalin!

Following the election, a year of terror began. One of the first impositions upon the Latvian citizenry was the devaluation of our currency. All private bank accounts were taken over by the Soviet Government. The next step was to nationalize all private property. Overnight, for all practical purposes, we lost all our savings and property. Now, everything belonged to the government.

I was fifteen and in my third year in gymnasium. That fall, our beloved gymnasium director, Arturs Lejnieks, was removed and replaced by a seventeen-year-old Communist just released from prison by the Soviets. He was not only director in charge of all students and teaching staff, but he also taught Marxist Theory once a week in each class.

Our new director had never even attended school. Still, his authority stemmed from his knowledge of Marxism, bolstered by the right arm of the Secret Police, known as the NKVD. A single word against Communism could easily cost one his freedom or even his life. We all feared the director and avoided him as much as we could.

Fear and Distrust Spread through the Country

On the home front, our lives had changed too. A friend's father would be arrested, or sentenced, or would just disappear into the night. No one was safe. It didn't take long before we began to fear and distrust each other, knowing a word that might be misunderstood could reach the ear of authority. We spoke in whispers, if at all.

Religion, of course, was removed from the schools, and our weekly religion classes were discontinued abruptly. In our gymnasium, there had been a Lutheran pastor, a Catholic priest, a Russian Orthodox priest, and a rabbi, each of whom conducted a one-hour class every week. Students attended the particular class that reflected their respective denominations. We were accustomed to daily assemblies held each morning in the auditorium. There, a short prayer would be offered by one of the clergy. Now, that was over.

Churches were attacked, and some were converted into libraries or Communist youth centers called Sarkanais Stūrītis or the Red Corner. In the Soviet Union following the revolution of 1917, all churches had been closed and their clergy disappeared. We all feared this would happen again. Soon, churches became overcrowded with parishioners seeking to baptize their children, confirm their teenagers, and get themselves married whether or not they were ready.

In the Evangelical Lutheran Church, our custom was to be confirmed at around age eighteen or nineteen, just around the time of graduation from gymnasium. Those who had stopped school after grade school were confirmed earlier. When I was fifteen my parents decided to have me confirmed before all the churches were closed. Besides that, my father's previous occupation as a police officer rendered him a likely target for Communist arrest, which could come anytime, and his future was very uncertain.

Under normal circumstances, confirmation was accompanied by a big family celebration, but these circumstances were hardly "normal." Even so, I took my religion very seriously and attended evening confirmation classes given by our pastor, Professor Alberts Freijs, at St. Peter's Evangelical Lutheran Church, erected in 1208. Local Communists would often throw stones at us as we entered the church through a side door.

My Confirmation Day at St. Peter's Church in Riga
October 13, 1940

By this time, Mami was almost bedridden, having suffered a nervous breakdown. Her medical care had cost quite a lot in spite of our socialized medicine. My father had no job at this point, and our resources were meager, at best. So I asked Tante Effie to help me prepare for my confirmation. On the big day, I wore a beautiful white gown. Tante Effie contributed the material and paid for the dressmaker.

After the church ceremony, my dear cousin Zigismunds (Zigi) presented me with a dozen of the most beautiful pale yellow roses and the book of Latvian Poetry I still treasure today. The inscription in the book is a quote from the Latvian poet Jānis Poruks.

> *Ir daudz pie debesīm zvaigžņu,*
> *Un katra savādi mirdz—*

Translated, it says:

> There are many stars in the sky,
> And each one glows differently—

After church, we went home, and Tante Effie prepared a little lunch. There were no more than ten of us, and this was certainly not the elaborate party a mother would have given her daughter on this special day. But Dad brought up from the cellar a fifteen-year-old raspberry wine he had saved for a special occasion. This was the first time in my life I was permitted to have an alcoholic drink. I remember how good it tasted and how quickly it went to my head. It was, indeed, a very special day.

Times were extreme and difficult for everyone in our country, but especially for men like my father who had been a police officer during the years of Latvia's independence. A nonsoldier citizen involved in law enforcement in the past was now considered an enemy of the people. So we lived in constant fear of persecution, arrest, or worse. The family of a law enforcement officer was considered complicit by extension. So it was not just my father's safety at risk; it was that of my entire family.

For a while, my dad and a handful of his fellow law enforcement officers found minimal jobs at minimum wage outside of Riga. But that was only temporary and provided no steady income. To make ends meet, Mother began selling her jewelry, piece by piece, to pay for my school and my music studies. She always stressed the importance of education and had chosen the best schools for me to attend. She would sometimes say, "Gerdiņa, we are not rich, and you are not a beauty. The only way to excel in life and among your peers is through personal achievements."

Our 13 confirmands and Pastor Professor Alberts Freijs

Departure from Riga

The Year of Terror

The year 1940 was one of terror. We called it our Baigais Gads. Thousands of innocent people were arrested or simply disappeared in the night because they did not agree with the communist doctrine and form of government. Latvian patriots—all of them.

Their nation was a small one built upon ruins left over from WWI, and it was a new and struggling democracy. Just over twenty years had passed since the war in 1917 and Latvia's independence the following year. The recovery period in the early 1920s after Latvia finally became independent had been very difficult for our new country. So much had to be rebuilt, having been destroyed during the war. Farmland had been neglected because many farmers had fled into Russia at the start of the war, in fear of the oncoming German Army. The Czarist government had also evacuated important industrial factories, government agencies, schools; and many people alone had fled deep into Russia along with their private enterprises. That war had taken its toll. But these Latvian refugees, including young men who had served in the czar army, were now returning home to begin a new life.

A wave toward independence—more of a "right wing" nationalism—swept Europe after "the war of all wars" had ended. Latvia was no exception. Its declaration of independence in 1918 established a democratic republic that lasted only sixteen years. On May 15, 1934, the government was taken over in a bloodless, overnight coup d'état by a group of Latvian statesmen supported by army generals and led by Kārlis Ulmanis.

Ulmanis, the son of a well-to-do landowner/farmer, was a Latvian patriot educated in Latvia and the USA before the war. A member of the Latvian Farmers Party (Zemnieku Partija), his slogan was "Latvia for Latvians and Latvians for Latvia." The all-party system and free elections of the Democratic Republic were dissolved under his leadership as were some international organizations. During his tenure, President Ulmanis replaced the International Boy Scouts with a new youth organization known as "Mazpulki."

I was nine years old and just entering my own formative years when Ulmanis took over the government and became our leader (Mūsu Vadonis). I was shaped in some ways by his ideologies and became an enthusiastic admirer and follower. My mother was always interested in politics, and she would often point out to me the shortcomings and wrongdoings of government leaders. This led to heated discussions between us. As far back as my memory goes, I never disagreed with my mother nor fought to defend my own views. And God forbid I'd ever talk back to her! Never, except when I had to defend my President Ulmanis.

In Latvia, there was a significant minority population that included Germans, Russians, Poles, and other nationalities. The president's goal was to unify Latvia by having those citizens whose names sounded "foreign" change them to Latvian. Our own family name—Podostrojecs—was viewed with disdain by many eager nationalists, a problem my father had already experienced. So just before the beginning of the war, my parents had our name changed to Roze. Its diminutive form, Rozit (the little roze) was my mother's maiden name. As it turned out, the name change was a good move, likely saving us from unnecessary questioning and maybe even arrests by the Soviet regime whose NKVD might have even discovered my grandfather's career serving the Czar.

In any case, the ideology to pursue extreme nationalism in the country met with opposition from social democrats and other left wing groups. Even so, under the "soft dictatorship" of Kārlis Ulmanis, our country continued to grow and prosper until the Soviet Invasion in 1940. Wondrous changes had taken place as the consequence of hard work and deep patriotic devotion. A significant shift had occurred, and tiny Latvia had grown into a flourishing new country, able to stand on her own.

June 14, 1941, was a day of infamy in our country's history. Thousands upon thousands of Latvians were arrested, taken from their homes, or caught in the streets and deported in cattle cars to slave labor camps in Siberia. The Communists made no distinction between old and young, men and women. Entire families were arrested and shipped out, often not even permitted to stay together. Men, women, and children were separated into respective groups going to various destinations in Siberia. Everyone lived in fear.

Mother packed a handbag for me and one for herself, in case the NKVD came to arrest us. She would stand behind the curtain watching the traffic in front of our house. If a vehicle slowed or—God forbid—stopped, we were paralyzed with fear until it drove away.

There was no one to provide advice as to whether we should stay in our homes, spend time on the streets, or leave Riga and hide in the country. Rumors circulated that there were farmers willing to provide safe haven, but there were no certain solutions.

The same dilemma held true for our entire nation. As the German Army approached our borders, the Communists began to retreat. But they were determined to destroy as many of us as they could—and quickly—before the Germans arrived. During the final weeks of the Soviet occupation, the Soviets intensified their arrests, persecutions, and torture of our people, ordering mass deportations.

My father hid with friends in the countryside and moved from place to place, as necessary, to keep himself unnoticed and safe. I saw little of him during that year. When Germany declared war on the Soviet Union, it took less than a week for German troops to cross our borders on their way into Russia, arriving on July 1 of 1941. The arrival in our country of the German Army freed us physically from the Red regime and, in doing so, saved many lives. But as it happened, this rescue was purely coincidental and was not by intent or design. We had actually greeted the Germans with flowers, but liberation was not their objective. Our euphoria was short-lived and followed by three-and-a-half years of wartime occupation.

Shortly after the Germans occupied Latvia, Father rejoined law enforcement. But things were not the same as they had been. His behavior and lifestyle had changed through these years. He withdrew from us and our friends. He had found new friends in the country where he spent time, rarely coming home. It had been difficult for us—even more so when Father disappeared one day, never again to return. He had found a new home, and I saw him only occasionally after that, at his "new address."

By the summer of 1944, the Red Army was again approaching our borders while German radio blasted with announcements that victory was close. There was always that mysterious message: "We have a secret weapon to win the war and beat the Allied Forces." Although there were hopeful signs that the end of war was near, we lived in fear. What was going to happen to us? The possibilities for escape were few: build a boat to try to cross the Baltic to Sweden, or try to flee into Germany.

There were some Latvians secretly building boats to take refugees to Sweden. Such an undertaking was very risky because the Baltic coast was heavily guarded by Germans. The other danger was the Baltic itself, which could be a very rough sea. Many rescuers lost their lives attempting to cross it. Nevertheless, the undertaking of this ambitious venture inspired fleeing en masse on the part of the Latvian citizenry.

One day, in the midst of this turmoil, a German soldier rang our doorbell. He told us he was sent by a friend of ours to help us with whatever we needed. He was about to leave for Germany on sick leave and proposed to take with him some money we might want him to deposit into a bank or to leave with his parents so we would have something to begin our new lives in Germany should that be our plan. He promised we would get our money back should we decide not to flee or find it unnecessary for some reason, and he gave us his parents' address.

This was, of course, a big risk for us. On the other hand, it was exactly the kind of opportunity we needed to take advantage of. So Mother entrusted him with two thousand Deutsche Marks, which was a lot of money in 1944.

A couple of months went by, and the enemy came closer. By the end of July, we were surrounded by the Red Army with nowhere to go but the open sea. Resolving never again to live under Communism, we finally fled to Germany although we feared that Germany was not winning the war as they claimed. It was a time of turmoil, marked by fear of the Russians, fear of what the next day would bring, and fear of our ultimate demise. We were plagued by worry about what would happen to us and whether we would survive or die in Siberia.

Nonetheless, my mother guided me confidently through all of it. I was her life's fulfillment, and she lived her dreams and aspirations through me. As an only child, I had spent all my early years with her. Now that it was time to begin my own life, circumstances allowed for no separation though this served to strengthen our bond.

Mother and I Flee Our Homeland

On the night of August 8, 1944, Mother and I boarded a German transport ship and left our beloved homeland. Uncle Arthur helped us get on the boat. By then, my father had disappeared into hiding from the Red Army, and I'm certain Arthur would have come with us, if only the

Germans had permitted men to leave the country, which, unfortunately, they forbade.

Before I left, I managed to throw into my carry-on my precious evening bag, my opera glasses, and some family photographs. Refugees were permitted only thirty-five pounds of possessions, which is very little to accommodate life. My allotted poundage included the book of Latvian poetry inscribed by my dear cousin Zigismunds who gave it to me on my confirmation day. Today—sixty-plus years later—I still treasure all these precious mementos. But they did not follow me everywhere.

When we fled, leaving everything but our meager stash, we never imagined there would not be a return. Just before we left, Mother dusted our dining room table, then locked up the doors. At forty-eight, she was leaving behind everything she had lived and worked for, never dreaming our departure would be final. In time, it would become clear there was no going back, and she was gradually overcome with the loss. Among many other things, we lost all contact with my father. We could only suspect he was rounded up, together with every other man, and forced to dig ditches and build barricades around Riga.

Later, when we would start our new life in New York with practically nothing, my mother and I would discuss any purchase we made for our home. Mother would say, "You decide, child, what you like and you want. It's your home, not mine. Mine, I left in Riga."

A Postcard from Riga

It was not until 1947 when Mami and I were in Germany living in an International Refugee Camp that I decided to risk writing a postcard to let my friends and family know of our whereabouts. Latvia was no longer an independent country after the war, but instead, a Republic of the Soviet Union. From this point on, any correspondence a Soviet citizen received from the West would raise suspicion and inquiries from the secret police and jeopardize the safety of its recipients. They might be arrested and even deported for "collaboration with an enemy of the people." So I addressed my card to my deceased grandmother.

Six months passed when, finally, I received a response from an old family friend. She wrote somewhat cryptically to provide us with what information she could, and we learned that my father had been deported to Siberia in 1945. Tante Ella's oldest son Zigismunds was drafted into the Red Army and was serving somewhere in Russia. His brother Edgars had been arrested in 1946 when he was only sixteen and was sentenced to twenty-five years of hard labor in Siberia.

Exactly forty-seven years after leaving, I revisited Latvia for the first time in 1992. Edgars had survived ten years in Siberia and had been released in 1957 under a decree from Khrushchev, which stated that anyone sentenced while a minor would be freed. I was fortunate to be able to meet with Edgars on that visit, and he told me his story.

It was his third year in a technical high school in Riga, and some of the forty boys in his class organized several small antigovernment activities, printing and distributing leaflets. Two of them got caught, but all forty boys were each sentenced to twenty-five years hard labor in the coal mines. Only one, besides Edgars, survived and returned to Riga in 1957.

Three years later, in 1995, I took my second trip back to Latvia where I found a document released by the current, independent Latvian government. This was a transcript from the Moscow Secret Service Archives regarding the political prisoners deported to Siberia. In it, I discovered that my father was exonerated for crimes he had never committed.

On January 27, 1945, my father had been arrested in Riga. He had been sentenced before a Russian War Tribunal on May 5 to ten years of hard labor for "treason to his homeland." He was sent to the Norillag concentration camp for political prisoners in Krasnojarsk, Siberia. He returned around 1955 and died on May 8, 1977. He had lived another twenty-two years after surviving Siberia! I was amazed at his endurance.

Today, as I write this, wishing it all was just a bad dream that could easily end, I realize how emotionally devastating these events were then and are even now. After so many years, I still have nightmares in which I am fleeing or hiding from Soviet soldiers or being interrogated and tortured by NKVD agents.

Refugee Years in Austria and Germany

Fleeing by Boat to Germany

The Germans took on refugees from Communism—women and children only. We were herded onto rather small navy transport boats, together with injured German soldiers being evacuated from field hospitals. The only requirement was that we had to sign papers declaring our willingness to work in Germany's war plants.

The boat my mother and I were on was followed and even attacked by Russian submarines. But luck was with us, and somehow we managed to reach Gdansk (Danzig), a Polish seaport on the Baltic Sea. At the time, Gdansk was occupied by the Germans, and there, all refugees were immediately placed in temporary transit camps called Ostarbeiter Durchgangs Lager or Eastern European Labor Camps. From there, refugees were assigned work.

The camp we were in was surrounded by wire fences and guarded by German soldiers. I remember the first night when Mother and I slept on the floor of a large hall along with some 250 other persons. Hay-filled sacks, one next to the other, covered the floor. There were young and old, many nationalities, various religions and backgrounds. But we all shared one thing in common—we were fleeing from Communism.

As more and more refugees arrived from the East, we had to make room for them too. Many of us, one after another, were transported further into Germany on different trains headed to different cities and towns—all this amidst constant bombardment from the air.

Finally, my mother had the courage to speak to the camp commander and explain our "situation." "We are on our way to Vienna," she told him, "where my daughter is going to study medicine at the university." As luck would have it, he gave us permission to leave.

Next Stop Vienna

When Mother and I arrived in Vienna after having gone through several Eastern Laborers' camps, it was September and the city had not yet been touched by war. The Viennese had it in mind that Vienna would become the next "Capital of Europe" and would never be victimized by allied bombers. But the following month the bombing began. The U.S. Air Force came during the day, and the British RAF flyers during the night.

Upon our arrival, we immediately registered for work, as required in order to receive our food rations cards. Mother was released from work because of her physical and emotional state. I was placed in a manufacturing plant. Non-Germans like us did not receive the same food ration cards as the Germans, and food was scarce. I remember being cold and hungry many a day during the winter of 1944-45.

It was then that Uncle Arthur showed up in Vienna, having caught one of the last—if not the very last—refugee boat leaving Riga Harbor. The day after his arrival, October 13, the Soviet Army occupied the city. In Vienna, Arthur got a job in a food processing plant. After work, he would hide pieces of cheese in his coat or pants pockets and give them to me.

For a while, Vienna was spared from Allied bombs, but that didn't continue. By the end of September, I would leave for work in the morning when all was fine, and by the time I returned from work later that day, my room would be in shambles. Soon they stopped replacing broken windows—boarding them up, instead, with plywood or cardboard. Gas and electricity were off and on from one day to the next. Mother could no longer stay there. So I moved her outside Vienna to St. Poelten and found her a little room with a very good Austrian family—the Mitterhofers. On weekends, I travelled by train to see her.

We had brought with us a few assets we could sell and live on for a short while. So financially, we had some small resources. But the black market prices were unaffordable, and there was not much we could obtain with ration cards at more reasonable prices. So I tried to locate our 2,000 DM the soldier had left for us with his family. I wrote twice to the address the soldier had given us but was unable to get a response.

One day—I don't know just how or where—I met a young Hungarian girl from Budapest. She may have worked at the same manufacturing plant where I was employed. In any case, it was after work hours, and she suggested we go to the International Café on the Ring, so we did. The only "food" available in a café in those days was a horrible tasting Ersatz Kaffee—some kind of artificial coffee. It tasted so bad. I mean, really bad. Luckily, we did not need to waste any ration cards on it.

Fifty years later, I can still see the café before my eyes like it was yesterday. We entered a very crowded, smoke-filled room with noisy civilian and military people speaking various languages. Next to my Hungarian friend and me sat three or four young soldiers. Remember, we were only nineteen! We exchanged questions and answers, and they wanted to know where we were from. When I said I was from Riga, one of the soldiers took interest and began to ask me more questions.

A friend of his had been stationed in Riga some months earlier, just before the Russians had occupied the Baltics. "My friend," he said, "was helping out a Latvian woman and her daughter. He had reason to think they might have to flee, and he offered to carry some money into Germany for them and leave it with his parents."

I couldn't believe what I was hearing! "Unfortunately," said the soldier, "he does not know where they are or whether they ever got out of Latvia. His parents have never heard from them either."

It was positively unreal listening to his story, but that's exactly what happened. I gave the soldier my address, and he passed it along to the young man who had promised to take care of our money. Before long, I heard from him and he sent me our two thousand Deutsche Marks.

Our Second Flight from Communism

In April of 1945, the Red Army approached Vienna. We had little time left, and I started to question whether we should flee at all. After all we had gone through, that felt like the breaking point for me, and I was ready to give up and stay in Vienna. "If the Communists have followed us all the way from Riga," I said to Mami, "where else can we go?"

But Mami was insistent. "No, Gerdiņa," she said. "You are wrong. Because we have come this far and left everything behind, what else can we lose? We must go!"

Even as Mami and I debated this point, we packed a knapsack and small handbags, preparing to flee yet again. This time toward the West as the enemy approached from the East. There was shooting in the streets. Roads were cut off, and bombs fell.

During the night in the midst of this turmoil, Uncle Arthur arrived in St. Poelten some time after midnight, having made his arduous way from Vienna, mostly on foot. He was astonished to see we had not yet left. "What are you still doing here?" was the first thing out of his mouth. "How come you haven't left yet?"

So together, the three of us left St. Poelten, hoping someone would pick us up in an army truck or maybe a horse-drawn cart. The few belongings we had managed to bring to Vienna were left behind, of necessity. The wonderful Austrian family who had given us a room in their home promised to save for us whatever we left, and they were good as their word. They packed a wooden box with our belongings and buried it in their orchard under a tree.

Uncle Arthur and Mami and I—along with hundreds of other refugees—walked and rested, rested and walked. Somehow we managed to reach Salzburg where we were told the city was overcrowded with refugees and could not accommodate any more. Over loudspeakers, announcements were made to an ever-growing crowd of refugees to remain calm and stay near the railroad station where trains would take us into Bavaria.

It was the first week in April, around Easter time, and the weather was miserable—cold and rainy, with snow and slush everywhere. To their credit, the Germans were very well organized, even in the midst of the war's final weeks. They fed us hot soup and dark bread and took care of the sick and the children. For the first nine days, we slept outdoors every night. I found a spot on a cement stairway that looked like it had once led to an Air Raid shelter, now destroyed from the bombing. It was the tenth day before a train pulled into the station and most of us were able to board. By then, I had acquired a cold that later turned into a bladder infection that would haunt me for years to come.

The "special" train we were on did not run on any particular schedule, so we had to trust that the train engineer actually knew where he was taking us. Sometimes he would stop the train in the middle of nowhere. There might be an announcement of an enemy air attack and we would be ordered to get off the train. Low-flying planes occasionally attacked both the train and its passengers. There would be no notice of when the train might continue its journey, so we had to remain close by in order to reboard in time to depart. We occasionally saw passengers left by the wayside when the train pulled away, and we began to suspect that the train engineer was a "communist sympathizer."

Every inch of space on the train was filled with its passengers. At night, all lights were turned off except for a red emergency bulb at either end of the car, which made nighttime travel especially difficult. Children were hungry and cried for bread, especially in the pitch-black darkness of night when every sound only served to add a surreal quality to our uncertain, overcrowded conditions. Occasionally, the train would stop at a small railroad station where the German Red Cross or some other traveler's aide organization would be waiting with necessary food, drink, and aid.

Rumors began to spread that we were approaching Garmisch-Partenkirchen in Bavaria, a small resort town famous for its winter sports. Our train slowly ascended into the highest Bavarian Alps. With my eyes closed, it felt like we were rising into the blue skies themselves. But all we could really see through the train windows on either side of the track was the close gray rock of some of the tallest mountains on earth—cold, unfriendly, powerful, and dangerous—which left me with the ominous feeling of being unable to breathe.

Since that time, I have come to appreciate mountains as wondrous, but only so from a distance. After all, I grew up near the Baltic Sea where the water—though no less dangerous than the mountains—is always alive, and where the fine white sand of the shore is ever-inviting and playful.

Just before our train pulled into the station, we were told not to open the doors but instead, to await further instructions. As it turned out, Garmisch Partenkirchen was, itself, overcrowded with refugees and unable to accommodate more people. So our "unscheduled" train continued its route to another small mountain town—Schongau—which turned out to be our final destination.

Meanwhile, the Soviet Army invaded Vienna and St. Poelten. They chased people from their homes and abused many women and children, then proceeded to occupy that part of Austria for ten long years under an Allied Agreement. During that decade, we were unable to contact the Mitterhofers. We knew, of course, of the kind of horrible mistreatment citizens received at the hands of Soviet soldiers, and my mother had tried to persuade Hansi and her family to come with us the day that we fled.

Only when the Russians left Austria were we finally able to contact the Mitterhofers, and they sent us our belongings, including my beloved poetry book. Its linen-bound cover had wrinkled from dampness that had seeped into the wooden box in which it was buried so many years before.

Hansi was eighty by the time I actually saw her again when I travelled to Austria years later to visit the Mitterhofers in St. Poelten where mother had stayed. It was only then I learned of the unspeakable abuse Hansi had suffered at the hands of the soldiers. Her story of what she and her young nieces had experienced was hard for me to listen to, and even more difficult, I'm sure, for Hansi to talk about.

"The Red Army arrived the very day after you left," Hansi told me. She had tried hard to protect the two girls, and at least her life and theirs had been spared. Hansi had spent six months in the hospital following a brutal attack that left her crippled for the rest of her life.

"Oh, Gerda! How many times I thought of Mrs. Roze who urged us to come with you when you fled! 'Come with us. Don't stay here! When the enemy army arrives, they will mistreat you. They are like bloodthirsty animals.'

"She was so right."

Refugee Camps in Germany

The Allied Armies were confronted with an unexpected refugee problem in Germany. The country filled with hundreds of thousands of refugees fleeing Communism. Among them were many non-Germans who had been brought to Germany as laborers during the war. There were also concentration camp survivors and former prisoners of war—mostly Russians and thousands of freed Polish prisoners. In less than four months following the war's end, the United Nations Relief and Rehabilitation Administration (UNRRA) established Displaced Persons Camps known as DP camps all over Germany.

Schongau

The first DP Camp Mami and I entered was in Schongau, a very small town in Southern Bavaria at the foothills of the Bavarian Alps. Originally, the camps were comprised of all nationalities dumped in together. I was told, early on, that Schongau Camp housed twenty-seven different nationalities! Later, the administration separated nationalities—especially the largest groups like the Jewish and Polish. We Latvians were combined with Estonians and Lithuanians in the Baltic DP Camp where the living conditions were far from accommodating.

During the war, these barracks had been built by the Germans to house Russian war prisoners. When the war ended, those prisoners were freed although barbed wire still fenced in the campground. And that's where we were placed by UNRRA.

Altenstadt

Following the Baltic DP Camp, we were transferred to Altenstadt. This was a prewar military town where the German government housed their regular army units. The housing itself was a considerable improvement for us. Still, several families shared a room, seven to ten people in each. For privacy, we hung army blankets from the ceiling to separate one unit from the next. Although the living conditions here were far from ideal, we made it work, reminding ourselves that anything was better than dying somewhere in Siberia of cold and starvation.

The United Nations and, later, the International Refugee Organization (IRO) provided us with both food and housing. The rest was left to us refugees, so we structured our own administration. We elected leaders to serve as our guides, and the leaders reported to IRO officials.

Our camp had a population of three thousand, and there were a lot of jobs to be filled. Cooks, bakers, doctors, nurses, teachers, maintenance people, and others were required to keep things in order. I worked there as a nurse for three years until I was admitted to University of Munich to study medicine.

Although Altenstadt was a great improvement over Schongau, the housing was very crowded. Because of Mother's frequent health problems, she and I shared a small attic room. The room barely accommodated two beds. We did have two chairs, and a wooden crate served as our table. My bed was pushed against the wall under a mansard roof, and I learned to roll out from under the roof and sit up slowly to avoid bumping my head against the ceiling. Even so, this was almost like winning the lottery!

My twenty-first birthday arrived a short couple of weeks after we were transferred to Altenstadt. I awoke later than usual and alone because Mami had been taken by ambulance to the nearest German hospital. Her pain from gallstone colic had continued for forty-eight hours, and I was not permitted to inject her myself with strong-enough medicine to help. Needless to say, I was very lonely the day of my twenty-first birthday. So I celebrated by lingering in bed and thinking of past, happier birthdays.

Birthday Memories

The Fourth of February had always been the event of the year for our family and friends. My birthday had always been celebrated with two big parties. One was for me and my friends on my actual birthday. The second party was for the adults and took place on the Saturday following the actual day of my birth.

Celebrating my ninth birthday with friends and cousins Zigismunds
(first on left) and Edgars (third from left)

There was much excitement surrounding these parties. Not
just the parties themselves, but the planning and preparation for
them were complicated and fun. All my aunts and other ladies
invited had new gowns made for the occasion. My mother did not
spare any cost to make my birthday a memorable one. Very early
on, Tante Ella's husband, Provisor Arnolds Zīle, came to our home
to supervise the wine preparation and beer-brewing process. He
was a pharmacist by profession and reputed to hold the secret to
making perfect wine. Naturally, he was asked every year to come
to our home and see that the alcoholic beverages were properly
prepared, especially raspberry wine, which was a favorite although
cherry wines were also quite popular.

Uncle Arnold was, by nature, a detail-oriented person. Unlike
his wife, Tante Ella who never took life very seriously, for Arnold
everything had to be perfect. "Just go with the flow!" That was how
Tante Ella lived life. But Arnold arrived carrying a suitcase filled
with equipment. There were long glass thermometers, various
timers, and measuring instruments. He even brought along his
laboratory coat and donned this before descending into the cellar
with my father where all the wine-making took place.

The wines were made in large, round, glass bottles. Glass
thermometers would be stuck through the neck of sealed bottles,
and tiny air bubbles percolated up now and then. All this had to
be carefully measured and timed. He brewed beer for the party
in a large wooden barrel that was usually placed in our kitchen.

It, too, had a measuring instrument attached, as well as a tap on the side.

Uncle Arnold wasn't a drinker himself, except to taste his own brews. He'd become very amiable with the ladies—any of them—after the very first drink. After the second, he'd fall asleep and have to be carried to the nearest bed, accompanied by my mother on the piano playing Chopin's "March Funeraire."

This was quite the opposite of my father, his brother-in-law. My father often made fun of Arnold. "What kind of a man are you that you cannot hold alcohol?" he'd say.

Mami took care of the food, usually with very little help. Although it was always a sit-down dinner, I don't recall hot dishes being served. It was more like a Swedish Smorgasbord with cold meats and various salads comprised of cut-up vegetables cured in syrup and vinegar. Many favorite dishes were prepared with herring and smoked salmon. For dessert was the famed birthday kliņģeris alight with candles and accompanied by French Cognac for the adults.

Preparation for the children's party involved crafting party favors each child could take home. For the boys, we made cone hats with a pompom on top. The girls got flower wreaths made of tissue paper.

When I celebrated my sixth birthday, I played hostess to my guests in a back room of the apartment while Mami entertained their mothers in the dining room. The ladies were having a great time themselves and ignored my trips to the kitchen and back carrying small cups of tea. I'd watched Uncle Arnold and my father enough to know how to open the tap and pour beer into a cup.

When the time came for the mothers to collect their children, they discovered them rolling on the floor, spitting at one another, and behaving like the tipsy partygoers they had become from the sampling of Arnold's beer I had served. I can imagine it was a pretty disturbing scene although we thought it was pretty funny. Needless to say, I did not repeat that mistake.

I daydreamed about my past birthdays until a loud knock on the door interrupted my thoughts. A man from the camp handed me a brown bag. "Your mother asked me to give this to you. I saw her yesterday when I was in the hospital."

Inside the bag was a very large, very beautiful shiny red apple and a note: "My dearest child, I'm sending you my gift on your twenty-first birthday! Each patient was given an apple, and I'm sure you know how unusual that is. I decided to save it for you. Happy Birthday! Don't worry about me. I will be okay. Love, Mami."

That apple Mami had saved for me was the greatest birthday gift I ever received. It was the sweetest, juiciest, tastiest apple I ever ate in my life!

Geretsried-Foerenwald

Mother developed stomach problems soon after we moved into our next DP camp in Geretsried where she suffered progressive stomach pain on and off. Our medical facility in the camp in Geretsried—the Dispensary—was small and not equipped to deal with any kind of diagnostics. We had one doctor, three nurses, one registered nurse, two aides, and the luxury of eight beds.

Somehow, we managed to take care of our Baltic camp population of three thousand people in spite of the fact that medicine and medical supplies were always scarce. The doctor had only three "meaningful" drugs at his disposal: aspirin, luminal, and morphine. More serious cases were transferred to the next largest DP camp fifteen miles away in Foerenwald with a population that doubled our own (five thousand Jews). At Foerenwald, they had an operating room with two surgeons on staff.

Mother was eventually diagnosed with gallbladder stones and was having painful colic attacks that lasted for hours and for which even morphine provided no relief. She had to be operated on and so was taken by ambulance to Foerenwald. When I arrived with my mother at Foerenwald, my first impression was that the facilities were much larger and there were more doctors and more equipment.

The surgeon who operated on Mother for six long hours was a refugee from Hungary. I learned as well that Dr. Hassler was once a famous Budapest surgeon, and I was relieved to think Mother was in such good hands. But she was very sick, and sometimes we actually feared for her life.

Since Mother's condition was as bad as it was, I needed to be with her and had no transportation back and forth between Foerenwald and Geretsried. The hospital administration kindly permitted me to stay there, and I became part of their staff. So for Mother's three-month stay at Foerenwald, she had "private nursing care" while she recovered.

Contrary to my initial hopeful reaction, I soon began to realize that the operating room environment at Foerenwald was deplorably short of everything. It was still early spring and the weather was very cold, but the operating room had no heat. The nurses warmed the big room with a small electric floor heater during my mother's operation. Dressing materials and medical tape were rarely on hand. Nurses would cut out the cleaner sections of dressings used for one patient to apply to the next. I don't think Mother's wounds were ever dressed with sterile bandage pads, and the only tape used was commercial electrical tape! When she returned to Geretsried, she developed an open wound, and her treatment there, after months, proved unsuccessful. Ultimately, she required yet another surgery.

Medical School

University of Vienna

The war had put a damper on my music studies, and by 1943, I had turned my attention to medicine. While still in gymnasium, I had already become interested in applying to the University of Vienna, which was one of the top medical schools in prewar Europe.

Austria was under the rule of Hitler at that time, and to apply to the University of Vienna, I had been required to submit documents to prove I was not of Jewish descent. "Evidence" consisted of seven generations of ancestors, usually transcribed from church books. So I began to research my ancestry.

I was able to find seven generations on my mother's side, but on my father's side, things became murkier. During the 1905 uprising in Russia, his family church had been destroyed by fire and, along with the church, its records and the documentation I needed. As it happened, I was able to squeak by with only four generations on his side, but that was the absolute minimum.

Finally, in the spring of 1944, I was admitted to medical school there, and I knew my dream had come true! Then came our flight from Riga to Germany, but always, my aim was Vienna. By September when my mother and I arrived at last in Vienna, the University had closed its doors to all students except for those in their last two years of medical school. The need for medical personnel was critical in the last years of war, and my hopes were dashed. But my dream lived on—if not in Vienna, then somewhere.

In May of 1945, the war finally over, Mother and I had moved into the DP camp in Schongau. In September, I was on my way to Heidelberg to apply for medical school there. Three-and-a-half months after the war ended, public transportation had not yet been restored. Many bridges had been destroyed in the last insane days of the war; and now, to get from one place to another, you could stand on the highway and flag down a car or, more likely, a U.S. Army truck. While they were officially instructed not to pick up civilians, they always did, thank God!

It took days to reach Heidelberg. I travelled with a knapsack on my back and some bread and green apples. There were no restaurants open and no food to buy anywhere, except a cup of coffee or tea now and again although even that would be fortunate. That trip was pure insanity, but nothing could have stopped me. In retrospect, the fact that my mother allowed me to go at all was very surprising.

On the way there, in Tuebingen, there was a well-known University, so I applied there in addition to the University of Heidelberg. As it turned out, both schools received far more applications than they could accommodate, given the number of non-German applicants from other countries competing with German citizens who wished to continue their education. I wasn't accepted at either. I returned home disappointed and tired but undaunted.

University of Munich

The following year, I applied to University in Munich. Twice—spring and fall of 1946. And yet again in the spring of 1947. By then, the German government had declared a new policy that limited Universities to admitting only ten percent foreigners, with the bulk of acceptances going strictly to German citizens.

One day in early summer, I met a Latvian schoolmate of mine from Riga on the street in Munich, and I told him of my experience and disappointment. He advised me that giving American cigarettes to folks in the Admissions Office was key to bending the rules in one's favor.

So that was it! I thought. The absurdity was infuriating. I decided to speak to the university president myself and see if and how this policy worked.

The president of a German university is called Herr Rector and, as I would soon find out, was regarded as some kind of a god. I asked the secretary for an appointment to meet with Herr Rector and tried to explain to her why I had come and why it was so important for me to speak to Herr Rector himself. While she was busily ignoring my presence, Herr Rector, Professor Dr. Walther Gerlach, walked into the room and invited me to enter his office.

I see him before me like it was yesterday—a tall, good-looking man with gray hair and cold steel-blue eyes. When Herr Rector spoke, his eyes held me hostage. My heart sank. All I could think of was "compose yourself. Sit up straight and rest your case. This is it! There won't be another opportunity."

"Too many foreigners try to wiggle their way into the university with falsified documents," he said.

I assured him that such deplorable behavior had nothing to do with my application, and I produced my original gymnasium diploma and handed it over to him.

"Well, we have to think of our own people first, especially those returning from war," he said and peered at me as if waiting for my next objection.

"You may not realize that I've applied several times. Shouldn't there be some advantage for that kind of persistence?" I asked.

"No," he said simply and handed my diploma back to me.

I faltered a moment, realizing I might be losing ground with Herr Rector. I took a deep breath and said, "Please, could you tell me to whom should I give American cigarettes in order to be admitted?"

Herr Rector was clearly taken aback. He cleared his throat and replied slowly. "I believe there have been some irregularities in the past as far as admissions are concerned. It was the summer help we had, but that's been corrected. It won't happen again."

My student identification card—University of Munich

I got up and left—dejected, of course, but determined to submit my application during the following summertime. As it happened, I was finally admitted the next fall, in 1947, without even having to reapply. I had finally made it!

The first day at a German university is a ceremonial event, something that isn't customary here in America. On our opening day at the Ludwig Maximilians University of Munich, the newly admitted students stood in a receiving line, and Herr Rector walked around shaking our hands. He looked into our eyes with his steely blue gaze and welcomed each one of us individually.

"You are herewith a member of the academic society, no matter where you will be in your lifetime."

Wow!

III

My Life with Klemens

Engagement and Wedding

It was in Altenstadt where I would meet my husband-to-be, Klemens Dobrzanski. Klemens had been taken prisoner in 1939 during the six-week German-Polish War. He was held in a Polish Officers' Prisoner of war camp in Murnau, Germany, for nearly six years. In 1945, the American Army entered the Murnau Camp and freed five thousand Polish officers. Poland was an allied country with an Exile Government in England. So the U.S. created Polish Army units from these soldiers they freed by placing them under U.S. command.

One of these units was stationed near our DP Camp in Altenstadt, and that's where Klemens and I met. I was twenty-two when we met, and he was eleven years my senior—a dashing Polish army officer and prewar military attaché. He was the first man in my life and my very first love! We had no home and no country, but we had each other and a dream that both our native countries would be free one day and we'd return home to live happily ever after.

When we became officially engaged at Christmas of 1946, the German economy was in disarray and the black market was flourishing. The German mark had been devalued; everyone who had money lost everything overnight, and we all started from point zero. Suddenly, one mark was worth what it said on its face. Now, one mark could buy maybe a half pound of butter, where, before, the price of butter was six hundred or even eight hundred marks on the black market. Consumer goods were scarce, and with that came high inflation. If one could not buy a product because it was not readily available, it would cost more for those who did locate it because there were many who sought it out.

Klemens always refused to obtain anything on the black market, stating, "My officer's honor would be damaged if I ever turned to the black market."

Conditions being what they were at the time, Klemens could not buy me an engagement ring. On the black market, his army paycheck might buy two pounds of butter, and I was proud of the stand that he took in defense of his honor. So my mother helped out by giving Klemens two czarist Russian, 24 karat gold coins to make wedding bands for the two of us.

Klemens Dobrzanski   Gerda Roze
Klemens and I became engaged on Christmas 1946

In the absence of a ring, it was customary then in Europe to seal the engagement with a wedding band worn on the left hand, ring finger. At the wedding ceremony, this ring would be switched to the right hand to signify that one was now married. Klemens was not comfortable with this arrangement and promised to buy me an engagement ring as soon as the economy normalized. After all, this could not go on forever.

Preparing for our church wedding with all the trimmings was almost impossible under these circumstances. But I was determined to make it the very special day that it should be. There was a rumor that it was possible to get a U.S. Air Force nylon parachute from which a gown could be fashioned. A young GI was willing to sell me one despite the illegality of such a transaction. He set up a clandestine meeting far out of town in a wooded area where he handed me a small suitcase with the contents I paid for.

As you can imagine, my mother was horrified to think I could be arrested for stealing U.S. government property. But I was smart enough not to tell anyone ahead of time what my plans were for its use. I brought it home and engaged a fine Latvian seamstress—a fellow refugee—and we simply began to create an exquisite wedding gown. It was designed in a Viennese style with six layers of ruffles and short sleeves. With the abundance of leftover material, I also made several beautiful nightgowns and some summer skirts and blouses.

So now I had my wedding gown; but I needed shoes, gloves, and invitations. And what about flowers and photographs? It was early 1947, and Germany had opened stores based upon a bartering system. As fortune would have it, our Baltic DP camp was moved again—for the fourth time—from rural Geretsried to Kempten, a larger town in Southern Bavaria. There, I found such an exchange store, or Tausch Centrale, as they were called. At these stores, shoppers could leave items they didn't need or could live without in exchange for receipts to purchase merchandise there.

No money was exchanged in these stores, just items traded for receipts that were, in turn, used to purchase other goods. I don't know the valuation system that was used, but I was able to "buy" long white leather gloves, a bridal veil, and a pair of silver shoes, though, of course, I would have preferred white. But white shoes were not available in those days.

Our wedding invitations were printed on drab gray paper and looked almost like newsprint. Now, it just remained to find a photographer. Finally, in Munich, Klemens found one who agreed to photograph us on our wedding day in his studio in return for American cigarettes, which were a very desirable commodity.

On August 13, 1947, Klemens Dobrzanski and I were married by a Polish priest in a Roman Catholic Church in Dachau, near Munich where his unit was stationed. The day of our wedding was an extremely hot day, and the car we had borrowed from a fellow officer was, of course, not air-conditioned. We had to travel thirty miles or so from Dachau to the photographer's studio in Munich and then back to the church where the wedding was scheduled for 7:00 p.m.

Klemens took care of the flowers. He rented tall treelike potted plants with white flowers that were placed along the aisle from the church entrance up to the altar. And he didn't forget my bridal bouquet—actually, I got two! Here's the story.

I had my heart set on a small round bouquet of white flowers I thought would go well with the style of my dress. My fiancé, I suppose, did not really agree with my choice though he never said anything about that to me. But he ordered two bridal bouquets! One was a larger, oval bouquet of white roses, which was clearly his choice and far more traditional than what I had in mind. The second one also was white roses but was small and round, just as I had imagined. When Klemens and I walked down the aisle together, I carried the bouquet he preferred because I did not have the heart to reject my fiancé's wishes. Soft introductory organ tunes played in the background. During the ceremony, a cellist played Handel's Largo, and a baritone sang Schubert's Ave Maria.

Following the wedding, we had a big reception at the Officers Club. Of our seventy guests, sixty-five were Polish officers and maybe two or three of their wives. All the men had been prisoners of war or were concentration camp survivors, and most of their wives were still in Poland. I had no one to toss my bridal bouquet to, which by now was looking pretty tired from enduring the heat of this long August day.

As for me, "I could have danced all night," as the song goes. Shortly after midnight, though, Klemens and I said our good-byes to our guests and retired. The following morning, we left for the Bavarian Alps where we spent our honeymoon climbing the mountains.

Our Wedding in Dachau, Germany
August 13, 1947

Married Life

My first semester in medical school was about to begin, and I needed to find housing near the University. But half the city had been destroyed by bombs, so what remained was full and overcrowded, leaving virtually no available housing in Munich. I asked Klemens to let the soldiers from his unit know what we were looking for. Sure enough, one of his men was dating a German girl whose married sister had a small apartment near the university and was looking for a single person to sleep in. I'd lucked out!

The Hüttinger family, a young Bavarian couple with a small child, were lovely people. They tried to make my stay as comfortable as possible, and I tried not to invade their privacy. It worked! Except for the weekends when I visited my husband in Dachau or my mother in our DP camp in Kempten, this would be my home on and off for the next two years.

On the university campus, some buildings had been destroyed and others, badly damaged. So before the first lecture was held, every student had to help clean away all the rubble. It was hard work, but the prospect of being in medical school was really all that concerned me.

The lecture halls were overcrowded with two to three hundred students. And although I spoke fluent German, I had far more difficulty understanding it. Reading textbooks was close to impossible. I would have the same problem much later in 1955 when I attended Columbia University in New York. Speaking a foreign language is not the same as reading a textbook and understanding it, so my studies were doubly difficult.

I moved in with the Hüttingers and travelled constantly between Munich and Kempten and Dachau. "Best place to find me," I joked with friends, "would be at the train station in Munich." My permanent address was our DP camp in Kempten, Bavaria, a few hundred kilometers from Munich. Klemens lived with the U.S. Army Polish Unit in Dachau. Even the Germans were digging out from beneath ashes and were faced with a nonexistent economy. Their own men returning from war were starved, sick, and disabled from incarceration in prison camps. It was clear why the Germans detested the presence of foreigners on their soil, and it was impossible to plan a future or to set any meaningful goals. We lived in an uncertain world. But we all knew we could not return to our Soviet occupied, native homelands—Poland or Latvia, respectively. The Iron Curtain was drawn, and we were its exiles.

Whatever necessities we had in the DP Camp were provided for by the IRO. So the IRO took care of my mother, and the U.S. Army took care of my husband. Klemens and I loved each other, but that was just not enough. Our daily existence demanded more of us each than we were capable of giving. The burden on my shoulders felt enormous. This didn't feel like a marriage so much as an extended period of dating. It didn't seem to me that Klemens was nearly as worried about our married lives and our future as I was, but I believed things would change whenever we were able to settle.

Slowly, the general economy began to open up for us, and Klemens's monthly earnings began to have meaning. By Christmas, 1948, almost a year and a half after our wedding, Klemens had saved enough to buy me the engagement ring he had promised. And so he did!

He did not consult with me or take me along to pick out a ring I liked. He simply arrived Christmas Eve in Kempten and gave me a nice fat diamond. It wasn't what I would have picked out myself, but Klemens had chosen it and that made me happy.

Unfortunately, the ring was way too big for my finger. But Klemens said not to worry. He had already made arrangements to exchange the ring or resize it, if necessary. The Munich jeweler where Klemens had purchased the ring even agreed to take it back and return Klemens's money, if he wished. So we made plans to go to Munich together after the holidays to resize my ring.

After Christmas, Klemens returned to his unit in Dachau, and I stayed on in Kempten until after the New Year when I set off for school. Once there, Klemens was always "very busy," so our trip to the jeweler kept getting put off.

One final time, I asked Klemens when we were going to get my ring resized. His response was shocking to me. "I don't want to hear any more about this ring," he said. "Stop asking about it. There is no ring waiting for you. The matter is closed!"

I was stunned. To this day, I have no idea what actually happened or where the ring went, or why. This shall always remain a mystery.

Coming to America

It had taken nearly five long years until the free world was ready to open its doors to political refugees from postwar Europe. Finally, we were brought one step closer to an opportunity to leave Germany and start a normal life somewhere else.

The USA was one of these countries, following Britain, Canada, and Australia. The entry requirements were quite stiff. First, we needed a sponsor, a guarantor for housing and employment in the States. Then, we were screened by the CIA to eliminate anyone who was not "squeaky clean." Last, but not least, we had to be in perfect health. Even a little skin blemish would arouse suspicion, and the screening process would be put off for at least three months, sometimes longer. I had serious concerns about Mami who always seemed to have some medical problem. If something were to go wrong and her clearing be put off for three months—what then? I wanted to make sure she and Klemens and I left Europe together. Under no circumstances would I have left her in Germany to follow us later on. That was not an option, and I knew it simply would not work.

To find a sponsor was not easy, except for the few who had relatives overseas. So various churches, religious, and civic organizations stepped into action to find Americans willing to sponsor one or more refugees. As it turned out, a distant relative of Klemens on his mother's side—Joseph Panczyk—sponsored me and Klemens through a Polish-American organization. The Lutheran church sponsored Mami.

So in 1950, we finally came to America. Mother, Klemens, and I arrived in Boston from Bremerhaven in Germany. From there, we went by train to Pittsburgh, Pennsylvania. We were admitted to the United States under a special Displaced Persons Immigration Act signed by President Harry Truman. We were all political refugees, fleeing from Communism post World War II. For us (and for many others as well), this was actually our third flight from the bloody Communist regime, and we hoped it would be the last.

The Pennsylvania Experience

Mr. Panczyk, or Uncle Joseph, as Klemens addressed him, had emigrated to America around the turn of the century. By now, he was a retired steel worker and well into his seventies with a wife and five children, two of whom remained on the farm where he lived. The farm had likely been a working one when Uncle Joseph was younger. But now, his family kept only one cow. Nothing was planted, so there was nothing to harvest, and the farm had fallen into serious disrepair. Still, the Panczyks' home provided us with a roof over our heads, and they fed us, for which we were grateful.

Klemens felt quite comfortable in his new surroundings where he basked in admiration from his uncle and the rest of the family. They were impressed that Klemens had been the youngest military attaché in the prewar Polish army, with a diplomatic career ahead of him at that time. It was true that Klemens had graduated from an old military academy in Poland, and he spoke six languages fluently. But the war had changed everything.

One night after dinner, we all sat outside on the porch to cool off after a very hot day. We were discussing the day's events, and somehow our conversation turned to religion. Most of our communication with the Panczyks was spoken in Polish, and since my Polish was very limited, I felt like an outsider, which did not seem to bother Klemens. Mr. Panczyk openly ridiculed religion in general and the Catholic Church, in particular. He sounded to me like an atheist. Soon, it occurred to me that my husband who had presented himself to me as a good, practicing Catholic was agreeing with Uncle Joseph. I could not believe my ears.

That night, after Klemens and I went back to our upstairs room, I confronted him. "Klemens, tell me what's going on. How can you agree with your uncle and support him while denying your own deepest religious beliefs?"

Klemens got very angry at this and smacked me across the face. Nothing could have surprised me more. I was astonished, but it took me no more than a second to recover. Calmly, I said to him, "You will never have another chance to hit me because I am leaving you. I don't know how or when, but I am not staying with you."

His response was to take off his wedding band and throw it at me.

Leaving Klemens

Even by the time we were three months married, I had already noticed certain behaviors in Klemens I thought I had not seen before then. In his relationships with fellow officers—even with his best friends—he seemed to be somewhat untruthful. He'd say one thing but do something else. Sometimes I'd ask him why he would do such a thing, to which he would either state simple, "You don't understand," or he'd deny it outright and get angry.

Now, I became uneasy and puzzled over these things. But what newlywed as much in love as I was with Klemens wants to stew over matters like this? Besides that, we needed to work though there was no opportunity here. We had no money, and Klemens's relatives had none to lend us. They had no car, and the only possible way to get to Pittsburgh was by bus, which we could not afford. Our straits were dire, at best.

I called the Lutheran Church Federation, which had sponsored my mother, explained my circumstances to them, and asked them for help. Immediately, they offered my husband and me a couple's position in the home of a well-known surgeon in Pittsburgh. Of course, we accepted it and moved in with Dr. Wagner, leaving my mother behind to stay with the Panczyks for the time being.

Dr. Wagner's home was as beautiful as it was big. Besides us, he employed a cook and a gardener. They provided us with room and board, plus $50 a month for us both. I was happy to be in a city where we would surely find other opportunities in time. Meanwhile, I vacuumed, dusted, and did the laundry while Klemens helped the gardener and washed the doctor's several cars. Even in 1950, $50 a month for two people was extremely meager. But this had come from the church, and we accepted it.

The cook was an elderly woman named Sophie. She had come to the U.S. from Poland when she was a young girl. Her job with Dr. Wagner had been her first and only employment. She was very nice to me, and she and I became friendly. She confided in me that, over the years, she had "survived" Dr. Wagner's two previous wives, as well as the current one who was young, not much older than me. The current Mrs. Wagner did not seem to like me. She refused to give both me and Klemens the same day off every week. So we never had free time together.

On my day off, I would take the bus out to the farm to see my mother. But Sophie urged me to start looking for a job in the city proper and encouraged me to move on as soon as I possibly could. We were desperate, and I was determined to get beyond our present circumstances. After all, I still had my mother to worry about because Mr. Panczyk's family couldn't take care of her much longer. Given my two years of medical school and three years nursing experience in the DP camp, I applied and was hired by a private nursing home where I was assigned to the graveyard shift from 8:00 p.m. to 6:00 a.m.

Now, I had to tell Klemens and give Dr. Wagner my notice. Klemens, for his part, was very angry with me because the job required me to live in the city. I promised to visit him on his days off as long as he continued to work for Dr. Wagner. I was disappointed and confused that Klemens couldn't see the advantage of being more fully employed, but I was preoccupied with the difficult task of informing Dr. Wagner himself.

I was terrified that Dr. Wagner, having been gracious enough to employ us, would be very upset. I did not want to offend him or seem ungrateful, but there was no other way. To give up one's job—especially having been taken in, as we were—was not likely to be viewed kindly, but I simply had to confront it.

One night after dinner, I found Dr. Wagner reading in his library.

"Is everything all right, Gerda?" he said.

I assured him it was and then timidly continued, "But there is something I have to tell you. I was offered a job in a nursing home, and I have accepted it. Now, I am giving you notice that I will be leaving in a week as soon as I can find a furnished room for my mother."

Dr. Wagner listened with more composure than I expected. Then a smile came over his face. "Good for you, Gerda! That's what I call spirit!"

And that was that.

On my next day off, I found a furnished room near the nursing facility. It was on the third floor in a one-family home. Then, I made my last bus trip to the farm and brought Mother back to Pittsburgh. Klemens stayed on with Dr. Wagner, and I saw him occasionally on his days off. In order to avoid another outburst of his anger with threats to harm me should I dare to leave him, I foolishly thought I could manage to gradually fade out of his life. Of course, that's no way to break up a marriage! My thinking was unrealistic, and I paid dearly for that. It was on one of those visits that Olaf was conceived as I would later discover.

Meanwhile, at the nursing home where I worked as an aide, the residents became very confused at night and often would not recognize the nurses. Sometimes they would even attack us physically. The only solution we had for this problem was to restrain them by tying them into their beds. The job became exhausting as well as dangerous, and I was compensated at a minimal rate of seventy-five cents per hour. I knew early on that I would not stay there. So once my pregnancy was confirmed, I decided to leave Pittsburgh for good.

Uncle Arthur had immigrated to America about a year before we arrived in the country. He had been placed on a farm in Minnesota by the Lutheran World Federation and was, by then, a man close to sixty. Mami and I had kept in touch with him, of course, so I wrote him about what was happening and asked if he was able to send us some money. He mailed me one hundred dollars, and Mami and I arranged to leave Pittsburgh by train and go to New York City.

When I saw my husband for the last time at Dr. Wagner's, I did not tell him I would never be coming back. He had threatened to kill me if I dared leave him or if I tried to break up our marriage. For his part, he had done little to mend what was broken and was, instead, worried about what other people would say.

My mother had always stood by me, and she and I discussed my predicament. I decided not to tell Klemens of my pregnancy or where Mother and I were going. My aim was simply to disappear off the face of the earth.

So it was by night that my mother and I left for New York, fearful and desperate.

IV

New York City

The Employment Adventure

Our First Night in New York

In 1950, when my mother and I took the train to New York in September, unemployment was rampant, even in the United States where there was strong opposition to admitting political refugees into the workforce, which came from unions and other large organizations like the American Veterans. But New York City offered employment opportunities, and employment was the key to my future!

In Europe, after the devastating war, unemployment meant no jobs at all while here in American it meant only "little" employment, like what I'd experienced in Pittsburgh. Even in New York, unemployment was high on the list of major concerns, but there were pages and pages of opportunities listed in the Sunday *Times.*

Once I realized the American version of unemployment was defined by an inability to return to the same profession or trade where you'd lost your former job, the concept no longer frightened me. I was confident I'd have a job the day after I arrived in New York, and that's almost exactly what happened.

I hadn't anticipated that the day after our arrival on Sunday would be a work holiday. I'd never heard of Labor Day, and I was very disheartened to discover that I would be cheated out of one entire workday. Hourly rate at that time was seventy-five cents, so a day was worth six U.S. dollars!

The only connections or contacts I had were names of people I didn't know, given to me by friends and friends' relatives, as was common practice during the exile years. People would give out the addresses of friends, wherever they lived. You never knew where you might be in a year, and contacts could be very helpful. One didn't expect anything more than just a little advice. Sometimes, just learning where to go and how to get there could be enormously helpful.

At the first hotel where Mother and I stayed, we received just such advice. There, I met a housekeeper who gave me a valuable tip on finding my way around Manhattan. "Now, young lady," she said, "you will never get lost in Manhattan. Just remember, the city consists of numbered avenues and streets. All avenues run from north to south, and streets run from east to west. And one more thing, all numbered streets from west to east are even numbers while east to west streets are odds." I still find that piece of advice useful.

I did have the address of a friend of a relative. Her name was Evelyn Drust. She was Latvian by birth but apparently had lived most of her life in America. She was a woman in her seventies who had worked for the local German paper as a reporter. I had seen a picture of her; and the image I recalled was that of an elderly heavyset woman.

Mother and I checked our suitcases at Penn Station. One oversized trunk had been shipped by Railway Express, to be picked up later when we had a place to live. I searched my purse for Evelyn's address, but it was nowhere to be found. I realized I must have packed it away in the trunk that was being shipped separately. I searched my memory but to no avail. All I could recall was that it was Second Avenue, and it was a low four-digit address.

In Penn Station, there was an entire room filled with telephone books, each bursting with thousands of telephone numbers. These books seemed to be from all over the world, or at least the whole United States. It took me forever to narrow my search enough to discover that New York City had five different boroughs. I had no idea which one contained Second Avenue. It seemed hopeless.

Finally, we oriented ourselves and headed for the lower end of Second Avenue to begin our search in the one thousand blocks. Surely we could locate Ms. Drust if we searched long and hard. We stopped at bakeries, luncheonettes, and every convenience store that happened to be open that Sunday. I asked again and again, "Would you happen to know a lady by the name of Evelyn Drust? She lives in this neighborhood. A heavyset, tall woman in her seventies." Every person I spoke to would shake his head and the answer was always the same. "No."

I had no idea Second Avenue stretched for miles from lower Manhattan clear into Harlem and even into the Bronx. But I was twenty-five and determined, and Mami and I pounded the pavement together. I had to find Evelyn Drust if it took my last ounce of energy. With that thought in mind, I grabbed on to my blind expectations and plowed forward into the search.

By late Sunday morning, we had already searched for hours from the bottom of second up into the nineties. There we stood—my mother and

I—looking for a woman neither of us knew. How perfectly insane it all seemed in that moment. Church bells rang in the distance, and a very light rain began to fall.

There are moments in everyone's life when decisions are made that map out future roadways. This was that moment in mine. I was destitute, with a mother who depended on me and myself pregnant to boot as I had discovered just before we left Pittsburgh.

Then my mother turned to me and said this: "Child, this may be the most important decision you will make in your life. You have two choices. You can still go back to your husband and hope to start life all over with him. Or you follow through with your decision and don't look back anymore. Whatever you decide, I promise to support your choice, and I will do my very best to help you bring up your child."

With that, it became clear that we needed to find a place where we could at least stay the night. But there were no hotels in the neighborhood where we stood, and I knew we had to go back downtown. Mother didn't want to take a taxi and ask the driver to find us the nearest inexpensive hotel. It was her notion that taxi drivers had close ties with the underworld, especially in large cities—even connections with the white slave markets. She imagined the mob dumping her down some shaft and shipping me out to Buenos Aires to be sold to slave traders. I listened politely then just took my chances and hailed the next passing cab.

It was 1950, and cab drivers spoke English, which helped. I explained to the cabbie what we were looking for, and he said he knew a nice "women's hotel." The concept of a "women's" hotel was not something we'd heard of in Europe.

The Women's Residency Hotel where the driver took us was near the East River around the high seventies. Meanwhile, the weather had turned, and now the sun shone bright as the cab stopped in front of a tall building with blinds drawn in every window that faced the East River.

The driver asked us to stay in the cab while he went to see if there were any vacancies. Mother begged me, "Don't you understand? A women's hotel? All the windows covered in bright daylight! And now the taxi driver offering to find out about vacancies? If you had any sense, you'd see this man is making contact and not looking for vacancies. This is a house of ill repute. What else could it possibly be?"

As it turned out, we got a perfectly good room for eight dollars, including some meals. Our most pressing problem was that we would soon run out of money completely. We had left Pittsburgh with $50 between us, and some of that was already spent. The most we could possibly afford would be two or maybe three nights. With Monday being a holiday, I was already losing a full day. We still had to find something less expensive and more permanent. But that was our first night in New York.

Weeks later, when I finally met Ms. Drust, she was still employed by the paper although it turned out she was not a reporter. She lived in a cold water flat on Second Avenue, and she didn't even have a telephone.

My First New York City Job

On Tuesday, I was hired by Hope's Press, located on Thirty-Fourth Street near the Hudson River. My job was to fold paper boxes for which I was paid minimum wage. The woman who interviewed and subsequently hired me was reluctant at first when she heard I had a mother to support. Imagine her response had I told her I was also expecting a child! I pleaded with her for the job. Finally, she agreed, adding that I could pick up extra money by working overtime now and then. That sounded ideal so long as I got my foot in the door!

The first week went by, and I folded the boxes conscientiously, watching what went on around me. I noticed that each afternoon, some of the girls were asked to stay late. But not me. Another week went by, still no overtime. Meanwhile, I discovered that six dollars a day before taxes didn't go very far, even in the cheap room where we lived in a rundown rooming house on Seventy-second and Twelfth, as far west as one can go toward the Hudson.

The room was equipped with "kitchen facilities," which consisted of a very small electrical plate and a tiny table in one corner. There was a single chair and a bed that I shared with Mami. In fairness, I should add that there *was* running water. For all this we paid seven dollars a week. It was a firetrap of the worst kind. Narrow, squeaky, wooden stairs led to our room, giving a creepy sense of living in a scene from a horror movie. The hall was long and dark with a 15-watt bulb that dangled from the extremely high ceiling. I never saw anyone change the bulb, and I wasn't sure how they accomplished that. Yet, this seemingly unreachable light fixture was secured against theft within a wire cage! I prayed it didn't burn out.

Still, my forelady didn't approach me for overtime. Finally, I mustered my courage and inquired as to why she didn't ask me to stay late. "After all," I added timidly, "I was told there would be overtime."

Her answer was abrupt. "Of course, Gerda, there will be overtime for you too. But only after six months of employment."

My lower jaw began to tremble, and I held back my tears as I looked her straight in the eye. "I can't wait that long. I need money now."

I must have been very persuasive because she agreed to make an exception. As she put it, "You seem to be a good worker, and we need good people."

From that point onward, I worked many hours of overtime and began to earn as much as $40 a week, which was a considerable increase. That was in September; and several months later, just before Christmas, the owner, Mr. Hope, announced a raise of ten cents an hour to everyone.

He called us in one by one to discuss the news. When my turn came, he gave me an unheard of, fifteen-cent-an-hour raise instead of just ten and a promotion to "paper cutter" in another department.

From now on, I would report to Ms. Mary Rosenbloom, and that dampened my spirits a bit. I already knew that no one liked working for her and that she was considered to be a live dragon. But she was the boss, and she was getting an assistant.

I was pleased and surprised to discover that she and I got along fine. Plus, I learned how to operate a paper cutter. Soon, I became one of her favorite employees. Precision was the key to that job, and I was determined not to disappoint. I worked on a large manually operated heavy paper cutter with at least a four-foot long blade—a sharp one. The process required heavy physical movements with my right foot and both arms.

That first winter in New York was very cold, and I did not own a warm winter coat. So I wore my European raincoat that had no lining. On dark winter mornings, I walked west, against the wind, from the Seventh Avenue subway toward the Hudson. One morning, I met Minnie, our forelady, going to work, and she noticed the thin coat that I wore. Next morning, she brought me a winter coat, for which I'll always be grateful.

Meanwhile, my pregnancy became perfectly apparent to my coworkers in spite of the fact that I spoke very little to anyone about my personal life. Everyone could see I had a lot to learn if I were to survive New York City. They became very kind to me, with advice and tips on where to go for goods and supplies that could be purchased at the least cost. At lunch time, we would sit together, and I learned quite a lot just from listening to them talk.

One elderly man whose name was Mandell advised me not to stay with Hope's after my baby was born. He assured me I would never make any money there and suggested, instead, that I ought to go to the garment section of the city. "That's where the money is," he told me. "It's piecework, and that's the answer!" He added, "I should have done that when I was young, but now it's too late for me."

I tried to listen intently to the advice he and others offered me. But my pregnancy was very difficult—maybe even more so emotionally than physically because I was very unhappy. I was constantly nauseous, still very heartbroken, and living in constant fear that Klemens would find me and harm me as he had sworn to do. We had no money to speak of although my mother helped us both to survive on the minimal amount that we had.

Sometimes, she and I shared a single potato for dinner. I suppose it's the worst situations that demand the most strength, and somehow we managed.

Our most pressing need was to move from the dangerous boarding house where we lived. But my wages just weren't enough to accommodate. We decided to write Uncle Arthur and ask him to come to New York and see if, together, we could all make this work.

In late October of 1950, Arthur arrived. By profession, he was an electrical engineer, but he was willing to take any job. He had a reputation for having been born under a lucky star, and it seemed he had carried that luck with him to New York. Soon, he found a job at FAO Schwarz on Fifth Avenue, where he was hired for a seasonal job in shipping, and soon after the holidays, they offered him full-time work in the repair shop.

Although Arthur spoke Latvian, German, and Russian, he spoke almost no English. Fortunately, FAO Schwarz, at that time, had many old-time German employees, and communication, therefore, was no problem. With Arthur's engineering knowledge and as time went on, he would set up electrical trains in the FAO Schwarz store and, for customers, right in their homes.

During my seven months at Hope's Press, I became quite ill during my fifth month of pregnancy and nearly lost my baby as well as my life. But I continued on beyond my eighth month when, one night, I was taken to the hospital. There, at four in the morning, my son Egil Olaf was delivered by cesarean section.

When Olaf was born in 1951, Mary Rosenbloom, my boss at Hope's, paid me a visit with gifts for the baby. Clearly she expected me to return to my job, but I promised her nothing. I knew I would never again cut papers at Hope's. Instead, I intended to take Mandell's advice to seek a job in the garment section.

As I slowly recuperated from my surgery, I reacquainted myself with the Sunday *Times* employment pages and watched for Help Wanted signs in store windows. "Experienced Operators Needed. Can earn $2.40 an hour on piecework." That was the ad for me, and I decided that's where I'd head as soon as I could return to work. Of course, "experienced" didn't actually describe my personal familiarity with sewing machines that bore no resemblance to our Singer machine at home.

I took a few lessons from a woman in New Jersey, who ran a kind of sewing machine operator's school in her basement. She'd had a shop there at one time with about ten sewing machines. She advertised her school in the German language newspaper, targeting greenhorns like me. So I learned a bit about how these machines worked and picked up practical tips on how to approach these employers.

"Whenever the employer asks what kind of items you've made, pick anything other than what they're working on. That way, you can be sure the forelady will show you exactly what they expect. If they make blouses, tell them you worked on pillowcases. If they do pillowcases, tell them you made pocketbook linings."

Heading for the Big Time

Five weeks after my son was born, and armed with some training and advice, I headed to the garment section for the big time! I took the ad with me, of course, because the $2.40 per hour wages it claimed reflected a very high number in those days.

The shop was located on West 23rd in the heart of the garment district. The interview was very informal, barely an interview at all. As predicted, the forelady, Clara, asked me what line I worked on before. I could see they were making sleeping bags for the U.S. Army, so I told her I'd worked on pocketbooks.

She explained to me that the first week I'd be paid a guaranteed $1 per hour and after that I'd be on my own. I would have agreed to anything.

"Right now," Clara said, "I have no free machine. But if you'd care to stick around for a while, someone will leave and you're hired."

As it turned out, my wait was just half an hour when Clara called me in. She and I entered a very large space—probably the entire floor of the building—with hundreds of sewing machines in long rows. Each row stretched from one side of the room to the opposite wall, with at least twenty machines. All of them were connected to a single motor. The noise in the room was deafening.

Clara threw a bundle of Khaki colored pieces of cut material on to the table. Then, she sat down and made one sample piece and said, "So here you are."

I shook in my boots; my heart was in my throat. I acted as confident as I possibly could and pulled up my chair. When I'd sewn a few pieces, suddenly my machine stopped. The other nineteen seemed perfectly fine and continued uninterrupted. I tried to figure out the problem with my machine, but it showed no sign of life. I had to call in the forelady.

She took a look and said, with a smirk on her face, "And you told me you came with experience. I'm saying you've never worked in a shop like ours. So you told me a little white lie. Am I right?"

I looked her in the eye and said, "Yes. But please give me a chance. I need this job and I won't disappoint you." And somehow I must have persuaded her.

The leather belt that connects each machine to the main motor had simply slipped off. I hadn't recognized that because I didn't know where to look for this problem. It was a simple problem that happened frequently because leather belts stretch and inevitably fall off the motor.

The operators were supposed to call in a helper to fix it. The helper would turn off the switch for the row, shorten the belt by cutting a piece out, and then snap it back onto the motor and turn it on once again. But the operators never really did that because this was piecework and every minute counted. So I, too, learned very quickly how to snap the belt back on without stopping the motor. It was an unsafe and hazardous practice, but we all did it.

Dangerous as our apartment had been, the shop (and probably many others like it) carried its own dangers. It was a firetrap with no fire exits. The windows and other potential paths of escape were blocked by bulk materials and boxes of God knows what. Inspectors came every month or so, but they got no further than the reception room where they were paid off and left.

Meanwhile, I learned all the tricks of the trade as a sewing machine operator in the three years I stayed there until 1954. By then, I had become the second fastest operator in the shop and was bringing home between $120 and $140 a week—excellent income for that time. By comparison, when I would later take a clerical job at the Home Insurance Company, my weekly salary would be just $35!

At the sewing job, I worked with every nationality under the sun. Most were uneducated and ignorant. There was drinking on the job although no drugs that I know of. The people were tough and used rough language. In general, we all got along pretty well, considering how many of us worked in such close proximity. We did have a few male operators; but overall, it was a women's world, and I was soon to discover how rough and tough the women could be.

One of the girls was getting married, and we collected money for a bridal shower. Several operators volunteered to stay late and decorate the bride's work station. The following morning when we arrived at work, it was amazing how much effort the workers had gone to. Colorful wedding bells, flowers, champagne glasses, umbrellas—all made out of paper—hung from the ceiling, with a giant, colorful, papier-mâché centerpiece that dangled in the midst of the beautiful wedding symbols and which delighted the other women who thought it was funny and perfectly suitable. When finally I recognized this represented a giant male sex organ, I was horrified to imagine such a display would honor a young bride-to-be.

I came home that night in tears and told Mami what took place at the bridal shower. As I thought of the women I worked with, it seemed to me I had sunk very low. But we needed the money to give us some breathing space so we could move from the boarding house where we lived to the fifth floor walk-up in the Bronx we eventually found.

My Divorce

In the fall of 1951 after my son Olaf was born, I received a letter from a lawyer in Pittsburgh representing his client, Klemens Dobrzanski. It said Mr. Dobrzanski was filing for a divorce on the grounds of abandonment, which had "made his life unbearable." I had no idea how he had tracked me down, but I had to respond. I couldn't afford a lawyer, so friends advised me to go to the Legal Aid Society of New York. There, they advised me to get a Pennsylvania lawyer and directed me to one in particular. I didn't care who it was because I was determined to give Klemens the divorce that he sought, regardless. I had no interest in asking for support, either for myself or for my son Olaf. My lawyer, it turned out, had other ideas.

The attorney agreed to an uncontested divorce; that was fine. But where my child was concerned, I had to ask for child support. The mind-boggling truth had to be disclosed that, unbeknown to Klemens, I had carried and delivered his son—a shocking revelation for him, I'm sure.

This is what my lawyer related to me when I met with him in Pittsburgh on the day of the Court hearing. "It was a quiet day in my office," he told me, "when suddenly I heard some commotion coming from the front room. Next thing I know, my secretary comes running in, all pale and shaking all over. 'There's a madman outside who's demanding to see you. He's carrying on like a maniac, screaming and repeating again and again that it cannot be true. It's impossible! There must be a mistake!'

"When he was shown into my office, I saw before me a very agitated, highly upset Mr. Klemens Dobrzanski. I confirmed to him that, yes, he did have a son by his wife who is now asking for child support before granting his requested divorce."

Then came the court appearance and child support hearing. On my lawyer's advice, I brought Olaf with me. Uncle Arthur came to help us survive the train trip to Pittsburgh. My baby was only seven months old but cute as a button. When I entered the courtroom, I could see Klemens and his relatives positioned on each side of the hallway, like some kind of an honor guard. I straightened my shoulders and held my son close. I couldn't afford to falter.

Klemens presented his side of the story, that I had abandoned him and caused indescribable suffering. He had done everything possible, so he said, to find me again.

"And what did you do when you finally got her address?" asked my lawyer. To which Klemens explained he'd gone straight to a lawyer to file for divorce.

I admit to several weak moments when I wanted to hear that Klemens had tried and failed to seek me out and talk to me. I might even have forgiven him everything and returned. Then came the final card. Klemens denied that he was the child's father. He was certain of it, so he said.

My defense was weak. He had only slapped me once for disagreeing with him. Everything else had been only threats to harm me if I ever left him. Even so, I had lived in constant fear that he would find me and come to get me. I'd come home at night imagining he was lurking behind a building or in a parked car, waiting to kill me.

Klemens was ordered to pay $36 a month. For that, he had tried to deny his son. In that moment when I realized this was all about money, I vowed never to forgive him anything; and for twenty-five years, I did not. It was on Olaf's wedding day in 1976 when I finally was able to let go of the indignity Klemens had put me through that day in Court. The divorce papers arrived several months after the hearing, which I had to sign and return.

Klemens never asked for visiting rights, which saved me a lot of problems. But it hurt to know he did not show an interest in seeing and getting to know his own son. Olaf would ask about his father, and I would say simply that he lived in Pittsburgh. That we did not get along too well, and that's why we didn't live together. I tried to avoid suggesting the bitterness I actually harbored toward Klemens, and I truly believe any marriage that breaks apart is in some way the fault of both parties. But there were times when my mother made comments about Klemens that were unfavorable. I was her daughter, after all, and she was convinced our divorce was entirely the fault of my husband. Olaf stopped asking about his father, I think, because he didn't want to upset his grandmother. I'm sure he grew up with many unasked and unanswered questions.

There are times when I think about why our marriage broke up. There is no single answer. Even after all these years, I cannot find the answers. One would think after so much time has passed, I could think with my head instead of my heart and figure it all out. But no. It is little particles of experience that, together, build the cluster of life. To unravel all that takes a lifetime, if then.

Mami's Life in New York

Shortly after Olaf was born, Mother developed two hernias that gave her a lot of problems and limited her physical movement. We knew she would require yet another operation. So I now had to find the best surgeon and the best hospital in New York City.

The headlines of the day read, "Elizabeth Taylor undergoes a successful surgery in the Columbia-Presbyterian Hospital where she is resting now in the Harkness Pavilion." That's it, said the greenhorn! Columbia-Presbyterian Hospital and Harkness Pavilion.

I called Harkness Pavilion to make an appointment with a surgeon, and I was given to one Dr. Moore. As I write this now, I laugh at my own arrogance or ignorance or naïveté. But for whatever reason it then seemed irrelevant that I'd just "gotten off the boat," so to speak, hardly having warmed my nose in the largest city in the world, and that I worked on piecework in the garment section, having no money in my pocket and no medical insurance for Mami. Once the appointment was made, I looked up the hospital address on the map and determined we had to take the subway from the Bronx into Manhattan.

When we arrived in the doctor's waiting room, I noticed that everything looked very elegant. People moved noiselessly around us and spoke in halftones. Compared to the environment of the garment shop, this felt less like reality than my own imagination.

Dr. Moore was a man in his fifties, of medium build with slightly grayish hair and warm gray eyes to match. He examined my mother and told us the results, which we expected to hear. A risky major surgery was required to avoid more complications ahead.

Suddenly, he turned to me and asked the question that had surely been on his mind for a while. "How did you people get here?"

I told him my story, having read about Elizabeth Taylor's case in the news, and he said forthrightly, "You don't belong here. You cannot afford me or the Pavilion." Then, he added, "But I am interested in your mother's case, and I'll do her surgery for free. Now, come with me, and I'll take you to the Clinic Patients' Department in another building and register her there."

Mother's surgery lasted seven hours. Dr. Moore quipped that he grew a beard while operating on Mrs. Roze.

Following the operation my mother improved for several years. But by 1954, she had become quite sick and could no longer walk the stairs. Finally, a similar-sized first floor apartment became available in the same building, and the landlord gave it to us. Our former landlady sold us most of the furniture from our previous place, so we had a good start in our new, five-room apartment where we paid $65 a month.

Every place where I'd worked so far was just temporary. My goal was still to complete my college education, as my mother would often remind me. She always gave me that certain nudge that would overcome any possible hesitation I might have had on my own. We'd saved a little money, and leaving the factory meant losing income. Still, finding more substantial employment was a step I had to take if I was ever to get anywhere, and one my mother encouraged.

I had also met wonderful, sometimes well-educated people in the sweatshops—mostly immigrants and often German Jews. They'd all started exactly the way I did but never took that critical next step because of family responsibilities. Besides the financial disincentive, there was a further impediment to the kind of transition I was about to make with my mother's encouragement. An employer would still want to know what related experience and/or education I had.

At the city YMCA, there was a young Estonian Pastor who helped new immigrants with employment. He had established connections with some banks and insurance companies and so had created not only employment for himself, but a helpful pathway for others like me. With his connections, he could bridge the gap inevitably created by the stigma of being a recent immigrant with only factory experience. Thanks to the pastor's intervention, I was hired by the Home Insurance Company on Maiden Lane in the heart of the financial district in lower Manhattan.

When I went to work as a file clerk in the legal department of the insurance company earning $35 a week, I felt I had finally made it. The surroundings were very pleasant. In three months, my weekly salary was raised to $38. I had no business knowledge at all, but I learned everything I could from my coworkers and absorbed anything that would help me get ahead. I enrolled in the NY Business School on Forty-second Street and Fifth Avenue where I learned how to type.

Still, the income was not enough for a family of three, and I continued to search the Sunday *Times* to figure out what office jobs brought in the best earnings. I discovered that you had to be a comptometer operator to make $75 a week. A comptometer was a manually operated calculator, a forerunner to the electric one. So in addition to my typing classes, I enrolled in a comptometer class.

The comptometer was an amazing machine once you learned what to do with it. Most people used it only for simple addition and subtraction. But I learned the most complicated multiplications and divisions too. Like anything, though, one needed practice. So I asked for a transfer to accounting to work as a comptometer operator. My salary increased somewhat but not to the level I hoped.

I became friendly with one of the senior operators—a lovely tall lady with distinct blue eyes and thick short gray hair, named Catherine Mossman. In her early fifties, Catherine was raising three teenage children, having lost her husband some years before. She was a straight-laced church-going

Scottish woman who kept a stiff upper lip, no matter what. Catherine was active in the PTA, the Boy Scouts, the Girl Scouts, and her church. She was decent, honest, and unpretentious. She was who she was and that was that!

Because there was so much more to comptometry than I'd learned in class, Catherine was a godsend. In the fifties, banks and insurance companies were known both for pleasant working conditions and low pay. A couple of years after I began working at Home Insurance Co., Catherine left for a much better-paying job at Railway Express Agency in Midtown. And I tagged right along with her!

We became good friends and remained so for many years to come.

Mami's Dolls

It was Catherine Mossman who helped launch my mother's doll business.

One night, upon my return from the office, Mother told me our pastor's wife had called. Knowing we were familiar with European cultures and styles, she asked if we'd be willing to dress a few dolls in national costumes for the church bazaar. My mother and I hesitated a little, considered our expertise or lack of it, and decided to accept the challenge. The church would provide the material and the dolls to be dressed, and we would design and make the clothing from our personal insights into the cultural details.

We dressed these dolls in Spanish, Scottish, Russian, Polish, German, Irish, and French attire, and probably other nationalities I can no longer remember. I'd tell the girls in the office about our big project, and they asked me to show them these international dolls before I delivered them to the church.

Late in October, I brought in a box with the most beautiful dolls (if I say so myself), and there was quite an uproar. The women had questions and requests for making international dolls that could be used for Christmas gifts. Catherine stepped up with a yellow pad and sharp pencil and began taking orders.

So Mother and I both dressed dolls that year. Later, she took over and I became the buyer and supplier for our entire line of production. I would buy eight-inch dolls and materials in wholesale places like Delancy Street downtown and obtain authentic costume pictures from libraries and book stores. *The National Geographic* was a wonderful source.

I had no formal training in marketing, but I knew these dolls were exquisite. So I stashed samples in my briefcase and approached fine department stores and gift shops. The larger stores usually had assigned days for their buyers to look at new products. So I would make an appointment to see a buyer and then bring in my sample dolls. I picked Lord & Taylor,

Bloomingdale's, Abercrombie & Fitch, and smaller gift shops. The outcome was always the same: "Nice work but not for us now." I learned soon enough that finding a market for one's product was a rocky road. Unless, yes, unless one had some connections.

Finally the biggest break of all came for us! Uncle Arthur had a coworker in the electrical repair shop of FAO Schwartz, whose daughter-in-law was a buyer—Mrs. Bea Whiting. Without saying a word to me or to Mother, Arthur took in one of our dolls to show to Mrs. Whiting. It wasn't at all the nicest one. As it happened, it was probably the one Mother and I would have considered the least well dressed doll in our line. But who could blame Arthur? With his engineering mind, he wasn't a fashion expert after all. He saw us struggling and wanted to help the only way he knew how. And he succeeded!

Next thing we knew, Mrs. Whiting was buying up our dolls for the largest toy store in the world. FAO Schwartz sold Mami's dolls at one hundred percent markup for $7 each in the fifties. So Mother got half. The income was small, but she loved the work and it drew on her talents. She worked diligently to produce these dolls all year long though the sales clustered around various holidays. The first FAO Schwartz orders were for two dozen or so. But as time went on, they bought every doll Mother was able to produce, and that lasted nearly fifteen years. In addition to sales, Mother also exhibited her dolls in local and national craft shows and won merit awards.

One day, she received a telegram from Mrs. Whiting with a rush order for thirty-six international dolls for a United Nations ladies luncheon honoring the Crown Princess of Japan who was visiting the United States with her husband, the prince. Attached to the order was a list of nations to be represented by attendees. Mrs. Whiting indicated that the plan was to place a doll representing the country of each guest in front of her place at the table.

Mother was given four days to complete the order, and she almost refused it. So just as she had done for me many times in the past, I stepped in and told her that refusing it was simply out of the question. Of course, it would be an enormous challenge. Especially so, since there were some Latin dolls on the list whose complicated costumes we usually made only for special orders. My take was that you couldn't get much more "special" than this! I assured Mother that the two of us would get the job done, and I delivered the thirty-six dolls, complete and on time.

Over the years, Mother's dolls represented forty-six nationalities. On several occasions, Mami sold entire collections, and she donated one complete collection to the day care center in the Bronx and another to the YMHA where Olaf went to Summer Day Camp.

Once Mother began making over $400 a year, I was advised by a coworker of mine—an accountant—to have Mami file her taxes as a self-employed person and pay into social security. Not only was she working now at something she loved and was proud of, she was using her talents to earn an income and was happier than she'd been since leaving our homeland. And so began a small business that over a decade and a half earned my dear mother her $75 a month social security pension!

Throughout this time, while full of energy and ideas, Mother was not in top physical shape. It seemed every time we took care of one medical problem, another came along right behind it. Once Mami's doll business was underway, she was less inclined to focus on her personal health issues. She would get up in the morning, just like she was going to work, and the dolls would occupy her attention. She, in turn, was able to put her considerable talents to use.

Still, it was she who cared for my son while I worked, pointing out to me that bringing up her own child was a quite different responsibility than caring for mine, her grandson. With all her difficulties, Mother did a magnificent job of bringing up Olaf. I've always been grateful to her for that. I could not have done better myself.

Later on, when her production began to decline as the result of her illness, she had quite a legacy to reflect on. And once she retired, she was very proud of the fact that she'd earned her social security pension.

My Degree from Columbia

Just before I applied for admission to Columbia, the Second Presbyterian Church I attended on Central Park West and Ninety-sixth Street offered scholarships to four medical students. Another opportunity, I thought, to fulfill my dream to study medicine. But it was 1953, and when I was interviewed, I was told in no uncertain terms the scholarships were for male students only. It was the view of the scholarship committee that it was men who were head of the household, and it was they who required their support. There was no way a woman could support her family with a full-time job *and* study medicine. So I had to focus on a more practical objective, and I decided to major in sociology.

The School of General Studies at Columbia offered part-time students evening classes. I was admitted in 1955 with forty-five credits recognized from my studies in Europe. Even so, it took five years to earn my bachelor's degree—the last year of which I was required to establish full-time residency in order to graduate.

Those were tough years for all of us. My evening classes were from 6:00 to 9:00 p.m., two or three evenings a week. By the time I came home, my son was fast asleep. I ate and took a nap, and then I got up around midnight, took a shower, drank strong coffee, and began my studies.

Mami absorbed an unbelievable burden, caring for a small child. Uncle Arthur helped a lot and did so many things for my son and for me. As for Olaf, the poor little boy hardly saw his mother except on weekends.

As my fifth year approached, I looked forward to being a regular full-time student. But this also meant I must quit my job, which left me with no income for the next ten months. I had managed to save some money in preparation for this, but I still had to take out a student loan of $1,000 in order to cover my tuition, which was $25 per credit.

Eventually, graduation day arrived—one of the highlights of my life. I had reached my goal albeit later than I had hoped by a decade. The commencement ceremony was very festive. My mother was there, my son, Uncle Arthur, and even my girlfriend Eleanor Diviaczky. Afterward, we all enjoyed Wiener Schnitzel at the Café Geiger in Yorkville. My spirits were high. I believed the world was truly just waiting for me.

I was so wrong! The opportunities for work were very slim for a recent graduate with a B.S. in Sociology and no related work experience. One had to have a master's degree. So I had to proceed to graduate school. Money was running out, and I needed a job.

I turned first to part-time employment agencies. They sent me to companies like Lerner Shops to do bookkeeping. Then someone mentioned to me that Columbia offered a relatively unpublicized (and not very highly regarded) employment service to their graduates. I was told they weren't very well organized, but I was running out of alternatives.

Graduation from Columbia University
New York City, 1960

In the far corner of a large office space, a student sat behind a desk minding incoming phone calls from prospective employers. He had a large loose-leaf binder full of scraps of paper and notes that contained information from these callers, including the company name and phone number and the job they needed to fill.

He flipped through his notes until he found something he thought might be useful. "It looks like there might be something for you here," he said. "This is a consulting actuarial firm in Midtown. They're looking for a statistical analyst. But wait. Now, I remember. They wanted only a man. Hmmm. Why don't you try?"

He handed me the phone number, and I called the Martin E. Segal Company. I got an appointment and was interviewed by their vice president Bernie Backer. True enough, they were looking for a male employee because of earlier disappointments with women. "They are young, get married, become pregnant, and leave us." That's exactly how Mr. Backer explained it to me. But they were looking for a recent graduate to be trained for a management position as a statistical analyst to work in employee benefits.

After the interview, they gave me two short tests—one in math, which I aced, and one in English, which I didn't. Mr. Backer went over the results with me. "Math is all that counts," he said with a smile. "In English, you made a few mistakes. But if I had to take a test in Latvian, I would never do as well as you did in English."

It seemed there was one final question Mr. Backer had before making up his mind. "Do you have a boyfriend you're dating now?"

Even then, in 1960, I felt this question was too personal and had nothing to do with the position for which I was being considered. Today, no interviewer could get away with such a question. "No," I said simply. I was hired on the spot. I remained with Martin E. Segal for ten years.

Once I settled into my new job, I applied in graduate school. Columbia did not offer night classes, so I chose New York University. In hindsight, I should have taken a break from the five long and difficult years I was earning my bachelor's degree. But it didn't occur to me then to ask myself if I was ready for another two or three years of hard work. Instead, I rushed into it and somehow managed to earn twenty-eight graduate credits and to begin my master's thesis.

At that point I had exhausted my limits, and that's when I gave it all up. Never before had I given up anything I started, no matter how difficult. But this time I failed. I still hear Mami saying to me, "Gerda, you've got to get your master's!" Sorry, Mami, I've disappointed you. You, alone, always believed in me.

My Professional Career

Meanwhile, I worked hard at my new job and advanced quickly in the company's management program. Instead of the two years of training, it took me just one to become an independent research consultant, and my name was added in gold letters to the executive rostrum displayed in the company's reception area. A very proud day for me and my family.

At the time I had joined the company in November of 1960, it had about seventy employees—a highly select group of professionals. It was a great company to work for. Now, fifty years later, it has grown into a worldwide consulting/actuarial firm with thousands of employees and many changes in structure.

Mr. Segal, the company's president, knew every employee by first name. He had personal contact with each of us. He remembered employment anniversaries with personal handwritten notes attached to an expensive bottle of liquor for the gentlemen, and for the ladies, one red rose for each year of service.

The men had no problem exchanging their bottles of liquor for two or three bottles of their favorite Vodka, but some of the women felt the roses were a useless waste of money and would have preferred the liquor. I guess I was never a practical person. For me, the gesture of flowers meant more than money in the bank although, admittedly, our compensation was comparatively low.

Only the ten top executives were highly compensated—no more than 10 percent of the workforce. By the time I received my ten long-stem red roses and thank-you note for my decade of service, I was making less than $10,000 a year. I had to improve my financial situation.

Olaf was returning to college, and up until her death in 1971, my mother's medical expenses and prescriptions had cost me more than I could afford. Encouraged by good friends who knew my finances, I began to look around for another career opportunity. I was offered a position by International Nickel Company with a starting salary of $18,000 a year, which I felt I must take in spite of the fact that I was six months shy of being fully vested in the Martin E. Segal Pension Plan.

Then it happened. In less than a year, the general economy turned sour. It was the early seventies, and the U.S. government announced a wage and price freeze. Corporations began to cut back, labeling this an "austerity program." International Nickel was a Canadian mining company with two headquarters—one in New York, the other in Canada. Their first cutback was to close their copper mines in Canada. The second was to reduce the New York headquarters executive staff.

Since I was one of the last hires, I was the first one to go. I can still hear Mr. Rome's words loud and clear. "I just received from our Canadian office the latest guidelines regarding our company's austerity plan. You seem to be the perfect specimen for the new staff reduction plan."

Before I could process the meaning of his words and that they were directed squarely at me, he added, "You can pack your stuff now. No need to report to work tomorrow."

I was stunned.

"One more thing," he added. "Our treasurer has made out a severance check for you, which you can pick up now."

The check was for three months' salary—very generous considering I'd only been there for six. But that generosity was lost on me then. I was completely devastated and didn't yet realize a long full year of unemployment lay before me.

A wage and price freeze paralyzed the country's economy. Corporations stopped hiring because of economic uncertainty. I signed with several top employment agencies and sent out resumes to every Blue Chip company on the list of Wall Street's Annual Top 200. I received exactly three responses, each stating they were not presently hiring, but would keep my application on file.

After my mother passed away, I asked Uncle Arthur, who had been living alone in a small furnished apartment, to move in with me where he could occupy Olaf's room. With Olaf's return to college, I now had extra expenses besides my household bills. I applied for unemployment though doing so was very uncomfortable for me. It felt like charity, but I could think of no acceptable alternative. Uncle Arthur surely sensed this, and he offered to help from what little he had, just as he had done many times in the past.

After a full year of unemployment, at last I was hired by a small consulting firm on Lexington Avenue. The present owner of this company, Mr. James, was married to the daughter of the original owner. Mr. James interviewed me and made me aware of an unusual "situation," as he put it. While his father-in-law was now in retirement, Mr. James, so to speak, had "inherited" Carmella who had been second in command to his father-in-law since the company's inception.

Carmella was in her late sixties and still ran the show. She was bookkeeper, treasurer, personnel manager, employee benefits consultant, and was involved in virtually everything. Carmella was known to be a dragon in women's clothing, and here I was with the dubious good fortune to have been hired to be her assistant and gradually take over the role of benefit consultant for their clients.

A very long three months after I began this job, Mr. James called me into his office. "I feel very bad to let you go, Gerda, but things are not working out," he explained. "This has nothing to do with your work," he added. "It's Carmella."

This came as no surprise to me. And as much as I needed a job, I was very relieved to walk out of this one.

Following a couple of short-lived jobs, in 1976 I landed a position with Towers, Perrin, Foster & Crosby—an old Philadelphia actuary and management consulting firm with offices all over the country. This company dealt with corporate benefits for their clientele, where my previous experience with Martin E. Segal was dealing primarily with union benefits.

Oddly enough, several years prior, an agency had arranged for me to interview with TPF&C, which was then headquartered in Philadelphia. At that time, I was prepared to move from New York to Philadelphia, especially given how badly I needed work. But something the personnel director said to me then about the City of Brotherly Love just didn't square well with the lifestyle I imagined I'd enjoy.

"Keep in mind," she told me, "Philadelphia is a sleepy town in comparison to New York. We go to bed here at eight o'clock!"

In my office at TPF&C, 1985

Come on! I wasn't really a nightlife person, but eight o'clock seemed a little too early for my tastes.

Anyway, here it was four years later, and TPF&C had moved to New York. Undoubtedly, they lost some of their Philadelphia employees in the transition, and here in New York I was hired on the spot. I stayed at TPF&C until I retired in 1988.

Between my employment at TPF&C and Martin E. Segal Company, I had the good fortune to work for highly regarded consulting firms for nearly a quarter of a century!

V

A Final Word about Arthur

Arthur was easygoing. He never fought back, complained, or imposed his will on other family members. He always refused to take a stand on anything, which drove everyone crazy, including my mother who was just the opposite—always ready to defend someone's right to justice.

It was Uncle Arthur who served as a father figure to me from the time I was fifteen when the Russians first occupied Latvia and, from that point on, as my father's influence on my life gradually lessened.

Before the war, Arthur had always held good positions. He spent money as it came, believing that life was too uncertain to worry about saving for the future and that opportunities must be captured at the moment they presented themselves. He never remarried after his divorce from Tante Effie, nor did Effie, who remained by mother's best friend all her life.

When my mother and I came to New York, Uncle Arthur lived with us off and on. After Olaf was born, Arthur also served as grandfather to my son who did not meet his own biological father until he was nineteen years old. Arthur adored my son and was more than a father to him.

When my mother died in 1971 and I asked Arthur to move in with me, Olaf was in college at Colorado State University. Arthur retired from FAO Schwarz after working there for ten years, when he was close to seventy. After that, he got yet another job in a nearby electronics laboratory in Mount Vernon, New York, and worked on precision instruments until just past his eightieth birthday when his eyesight began to fail.

Finally, it became apparent that I could not care for him adequately and continue to work. Leaving him alone each day was dangerous, and we had no money to hire help. It was a very hard decision I had to make to ensure that Arthur had the care that he needed. His mind was still sharp and he wanted to stay with me, but I felt the only option was a nursing home.

To compensate (if that's the right word to use), I visited him every night after work, did his laundry, and brought him home for the holidays. I ensured that he was properly cared for by the staff at the nursing home.

His room was at the far end of a hallway, and as I approached his room every night, he recognized my steps even when his eyesight was all but gone and he had only his hearing to rely on. He would have a bright smile on his face when I came through the door to give him a big hug.

Uncle Arthur spent two years in the nursing home and died in 1977 at the age of eighty-six.

VI

My Life as an Artist

Gerda the Painter

During the sixties, I met Ria Kitchner when I worked at the Segal Company where she was secretary to Mr. Segal himself. She was a beautiful woman in her early sixties and had been with the company many years. Ria was very accommodating and always had a welcoming smile on her face. She had several good watercolor paintings that hung on the walls of her office. I was soon to discover it was she who had painted them. As Ria and I got to know each other, she suggested I join her for Monday night workshops at Ted Davis's Studio on Seventeenth Street. That was 1965, and it sounded just perfect!

The studio was on the fifth floor of an old walk-up. I'd pack my paint box and take the Fifth Avenue bus down to Union Square. There, I'd climb the dimly lit stairway where the wood made creaking sounds at every step. It was arduous and bleak until one finally arrived at the brightly lit studio.

Ted Davis was an elderly man who worked in his studio every day of the year. He was a casein painter, so casein became my first painting medium. While this is a water-based paint, it works just like oil but dries quicker, more like watercolor. His small group of students ranged in experience. I was the newcomer and only a beginner.

Every Monday when we arrived in his studio, the easels were set up and paints were laid out. Three Mondays each month, in the center of the room on a low table, Ted would set up a still-life arrangement—either fruit or vegetable. The fourth Monday, the decor would be a vase with a bouquet of fresh flowers. I painted with Ted for three years, and he never varied this routine.

I painted on heavy watercolor paper, which enabled me to roll up the painting at the end of the session and carry it home on the subway. There, Olaf and Mother anxiously awaited "Mami's new painting." For Olaf, it was surely an excuse to stay up late on a week night. "When are you going to paint something else," he asked one night, "besides onions and cucumbers and eggplants?"

I had to agree with Olaf. Twenty years earlier when I had attended drawing classes in my gymnasium, Professor Jānis Zvirbulis would guide us gently into practical applications of the exercises we carried out in the classroom. Maybe now I was anxious to recapture something that felt like lost time in my artwork.

In any case, after two years with Ted, I decided to look around and ended up enrolling in Sid Dickinson's figure drawing class at the New York Art Students League on Fiftyseventh Street. I stayed there several years. The classes were overcrowded and usually run by a monitor rather than Sid. A student was lucky to get a couple of minutes' attention from Sid Dickinson himself. Furthermore, I think I did not have sufficient knowledge to work on my own and probably needed more personal attention.

There, we did mostly figurative drawings of live models. How I struggled! During those early years of my art career, I seemed always to be searching for the right teacher. Then, I heard of "the Plateau Cirque," a small workshop in Bronxville, taught by New York City artist Donald Pierce. Once a week on Monday nights, the group would meet in the rented basement of a local church. Donald was a man in his sixties who lived with his artist wife, Rosalyn Stern, and their two grown children in the West Village. He'd travel by train to Bronxville every week to teach two groups—one daytime class and one in the evening. I became one of the "night people," so-called by students in the day class.

I stayed with Donald Pierce almost thirteen years, from 1973 to 1985. He had an excellent background for teaching. He was a Pratt Institute graduate and ran a summer art school in Provincetown, Massachusetts for many years and taught art in several colleges and high schools during the winter months. Don was an old-timer and believed an artist is only an artist if he goes to his studio every morning, spends all day there, and returns home at night.

Over the years I got to know Don much better, and I would have agreed with his view had he lived in the Middle Ages or maybe the Renaissance, but not in the twentieth century. By this time, there were few art patrons around to adopt an artist, commission him to paint, and provide everything needed for daily living.

But Don had a family to take care of. Or maybe I should say "which he ought to have taken care of." But I'm not sure that thought ever entered his mind. Sometimes it happens in life that things work out in the end. In Don's case, his wife—an established, successful graphics artist—stepped in and took care of the family herself. Rosalyn was employed full time as a commercial artist and squeezed in her own art work on weekends. And so, they lived happily ever after, until Rosalyn died one day and "The Rock of Gibraltar" was gone.

Don, for his part, was a strict, methodical teacher who believed each student had to find his own way. We used to say behind his back, "He enjoys making us crawl, rarely giving us a helping hand." Cubism was his forte, and I felt like I'd finally found an artistic place that suited me.

No one in our group of ten night students had the luxury of studying art during the day. We all worked at day jobs. Once a year, usually in spring, we'd have a big group show for both the day and the night students. There was always much preparation and even more excitement. I remember those early days when I'd see my works hanging on the wall. What satisfaction to see my creations exhibited there! For that moment in time, nothing else mattered—not dragging myself to class after returning home tired from my day job at TPF&C; not the cold, snowy winter nights with icy roads and my car sliding all over the place. Now, it seemed my arrival in the studio felt like entering an entirely different world—one that smelled of turpentine and oil. I was in heaven!

In the mid-seventies I began submitting my paintings to local art shows. In Westchester County, we have a dozen "women's" clubs that organize annual art shows. These are non-juried shows where everyone can enter with one or two works for a fee of five dollars. The club provides a reception and a juror to give out awards for the best works in each category. In 1978, I entered one of the Beaux Arts shows sponsored by the White Plains Women's Club and received my first award for a small oil painting in Cubist style, entitled "Sail Boats."

I continued to study with Don, but progress was slow. His personality was not easy, and sometimes he ripped my work apart. I'd come home in tears, having endured his "no mercy" attitude. Granted, the experience of other students was similar, and maybe that helped those of us who persisted to stay with him.

After five years with Don (and thirteen years since I had begun to paint), he said to me one night, "Gerda, I think you're ready to start planning a solo show. It's about time." The following year, I had that first show at the Bronxville Library, which turned out to be a big success! I was only sad that my mother was not there to witness it all. She was always the one person I could count on to support and encourage me. She was my guiding light, and we would have celebrated together.

Over the next five years, I became Don's star student. That's when I knew it was time to move on. I had to advance and expand my horizons. I had to learn more for myself and my future as an artist than simply to serve as an example for others.

I still had a full-time job in the city, so I looked for a class for artists like me with a day job. One of my artist friends, Rose Marie Cherundolo from Don's class, had moved on to a more advanced class under Harriet FeBland. Harriet's "Advanced Painters Workshop" at the Pelham Arts Center met once a week for a four-hour session, and Rose Marie raved about what a great teacher she was. The Arts Center was close to my home, but the workshop was four hours and scheduled in the daytime. I was determined to figure out a way to manage both this and my job.

Up until that point, my career as a senior corporate benefits specialist with Towers, Perrin, Foster, and Crosby had been of great importance to me. I took my middle management position very seriously and worked hard to advance to the level of senior corporate research consultant. I decided to take a half vacation day each week from my job and spend that time studying art in Harriet's class. I would still go to Don's class every week in the evening until I could screw up the courage to resign.

This plan looked good on paper, but it didn't work very well. I'd sometimes miss the train to Manhattan and arrive late in the office. Even when both the train and I were punctual, which wasn't often, by the time I arrived at my desk, I was hardly ready to turn my attention to work on my projects. The more I progressed with my art studies, the harder it was for me to wear two hats at the same time.

I participated in juried art shows, joined several professional art organizations, and in the ten years from 1979 to 1989, I had seven solo shows. Between my art and my position, life became exhausting.

The company changed, too, as new management took over. As the pressure mounted, I realized I had to make a decision between my art and my professional life—to stay in my job and continue to devote myself to a career, as I had for so long, or to take early retirement and devote myself entirely to art. A few years prior, I had purchased a co-op for which I took out a fifteen-year mortgage. So I had good reason to be concerned about my finances and whether I'd be able to manage.

At one point, I suffered from pretty severe headaches, which concerned my mother more than it concerned me. But she insisted I see her doctor for a good check-up. I had gotten to know Dr. Epstein over the years from taking my mother there for appointments.

He found nothing wrong with me, but prescribed medication that was a bit stronger than the aspirin I had been taking. "Tell me, Gerda," he said, "do you love your work?"

"Dr. Epstein," I told him, "I have a good job in a top-notch company. I'm well paid, and that enables me to take good care of my family. That's all I need."

He responded, "I didn't ask you to describe your company. I asked you—do you love your work?"

I reflected on that, both then and now, and wondered about the relationship of my physical ailments to the stress I experienced. Finally, in 1987 at age sixty-three, I decided to accept an offer to retire earlier than planned with a generous severance package. Whatever the financial disadvantage I believed that would or might be in the long run, the truth is I gained far more in the freedom to pursue what I really wanted to do.

I know one cannot expect to begin a new life at age sixty-three, but it certainly worked for me. Harriet's method of teaching would bring out all I had learned from Donald Pierce over the years, but which I never understood how to apply to the canvas. Suddenly, my structured cubist style loosened up into something more abstract and nonobjective. New blood pumped through my veins.

Over the years, I studied under two types of teachers—the givers and the hoarders. Some teachers give all they know to their students and don't hold anything back. Others lend a helping hand to their students, but only unwillingly. Harriet FeBland, under whom I studied from 1985 to 1995, was one of the givers. She used to say to us, "I want to teach you all I know. I am never afraid there will be nothing left for me. No, each of you will interpret what you hear and see in your own unique way and will apply it differently to your own work."

Leaving Don's workshop where I'd spent so many years was itself a very hard nut to crack. I was deeply attached to the group and to Don. We'd gone through good and bad nights—some with laughter, others with tears. We all had a common goal: to do better next Monday night. It was necessary to have that burning desire to create in spite of all obstacles. Some of us were better at that than others, but we respected each other and our individual achievements.

There had always been some animosity between Harriet FeBland and Donald Pierce—both wonderful artists with great influence on my art career. I wanted more than anything to part with Don on good terms but imagined his disappointment and hurt when I told him I was leaving. I postponed it as long as I could until one day I began to evaluate my dilemma by placing myself in Don's position.

How would I react if I had a student who was finally ready to leave after twelve long years under my tutelage? Would I resent it, or should I support it? The answer seemed clear to me that a fair mind would support the decision to expand one's knowledge and to search for new horizons, and Don was indeed a fair man.

It was 1985 when I had my first solo show of "After-Don" works. I invited him, of course, and he came to my opening. He studied my paintings, looked around again and again and finally said, "Yes, Gerda, I must admit, Harriet managed to bring out of you more than I ever could."

We remained good friends until his death some years later.

Harriet FeBland (left), Donald Pierce (right) and me at the reception for my Solo Show at the Eastchester Gallery in 1985

Gerda the Constructionist

Harriet FeBland was a constructionist herself, and she would challenge me to be more creative—particularly with the shape of my canvas. This intrigued me, and I began to experiment with crossing the border from a typical canvas to something that was not rectangular. This opened my mind to the discovery that one need not be bound by prescribed corners and walls. Now, I could experiment with borders, cutting them short, expanding them, or distorting them in various ways. This contributed a unique quality to the work I produced. I felt my paintings became truly one-of-a-kind in a very personal way.

Constructionism, of course, required new techniques. Screws, nails, hammers, saws, scissors, X-Acto blades, carpenter's glue—these all became very important to me and a regular part of my artist's tool kit.

The unusual shape of the canvas became part of the work and added another dimension to the flat surface I'd grown accustomed to. Taking a corner of one piece and layering it in some way to overlap another, suddenly I had a different way to present depth through shadow and space.

In the studio with one of my constructions

I also created diptychs and triptychs—a series of twelve such paintings over several years. During this time, our country was seriously exploring space, and this greatly influenced my work. So I named this series my "Orbit Paintings."

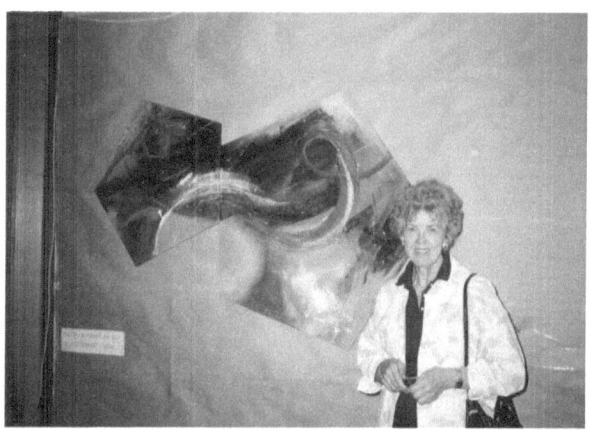

In Orbit diptych
Presented at the closing exhibition of the Master Art Workshop at
LIU in Southampton, LI, 1989

This also launched my love affair with the circle, which was the focus of my last three solo shows in 2009, 2010, and 2011. The mystery of the seemingly simple yet complicated shape of the universal circle fascinated me. When I used the circle as the shape of the canvas, the paintings took on a sculptural look that evoked the theme of eternity—the absence of beginning or end.

Gerda the Printmaker

Long Island University (LIU) sponsored month-long summer workshops known as the Master Art Workshop. This took place on its summer campus in Southampton on Long Island. In the late eighties when I attended, the program was run by Ann Chwatzky. The workshop was designed for artists to work independently with no classroom instruction. But big-name guest artists from the Hamptons were invited to lecture and critique students' works in progress. The summer I went, I met Larry Rivers, Robert Dash, Eric Fischl, and other notable artists. Some of them invited us to their studios.

There were thirty artists from all over the world who came to the Master Art Workshop. The studios in the facility were spacious and had skylights in many of them. As we each arrived, we looked for the studio with the best light. It didn't occur to those of us who were new that, as the hot summer wore on, the skylight would create a stifling greenhouse effect in the non-air-conditioned studio. Many of us eventually found it almost impossible to work without covering the skylight with large sheets of paper.

In the first week, we were required to attend a three-hour class entitled "Introduction to Printmaking," led by Master Printer Dan Welden. Thereafter, participation was voluntary. At the end of the workshop, an exhibition of our works was scheduled, which included one or two prints. This was an annual event in the Hamptons and was attended by gallery owners, art critics, collectors, important artists, and even the press. So we all held out hope for a contract from one of the well-known galleries. I believe one artist from our group—a very talented young painter from San Francisco, Robert Morgan—was contacted by a gallery interested in his work.

I had never been exposed to graphics before, so I was delighted to learn about printmaking. As it happened, my first monoprint was a winner. Mr. Welden held it up for the class to see and said, "Now, de Kooning, move over!" Although I realized this was only beginner's luck, I was delighted and thrilled with his comment.

The guest instructors critiqued our works a couple of times during the month we were there. When Mr. Welden's turn came, I pinned six prints on the wall for him to look at. His comments about all of them were uniformly rude and spiteful. I left crying, and he followed me into the next room where I asked him why he was being so unkind.

"Just to take the wind out of your sails," he said in a straightforward manner.

I had never experienced (nor have I since) anything so hateful in my entire art career as that experience with him. Even so, I continued to learn about printmaking there because I found it quite interesting. Even better, the graphics studio was one of the only air-conditioned places available to work. In the cool of the morning, I would paint in my un-air-conditioned studio until breakfast. Then, I'd spend the entire afternoon in the cool comfort of the graphics studio.

Despite my experience that summer with Mr. Welden, I still divide my artistic endeavors pretty equally between painting and printmaking, which, of course, requires a press. Back at home, I realized either I would need to find a graphics studio with available presses or I would have to rent work space.

That's when I met Louise Stern who was a comember of the Mamaroneck Artists' Guild. She was a printmaker in her own right and had studied under the well-known Brazilian printmaker Roberto DeLamonica for many years. Roberto lived on Staten Island, but taught in New York and in New Jersey.

I joined his workshop at the Northern New Jersey Art Center in New Milford and had the good fortune to work under his guidance for almost four years when he died from lung disease caused by the poisonous chemicals he worked with, as had many other printers. He was a wonderful teacher, and his departure was a great loss. Although I continued to work in New Jersey, I never found another instructor who could replace Roberto.

Residency at the Vermont Studio Center in 1997

I took a workshop with Clare Romano on collagraphs at Silvermine Art School in Connecticut. Then, I followed Clare and her husband—printmaker John Ross—to Venice, Italy where I spent a month at the Scuola Internazionali di Grafica, sponsored by Pratt Institute.

For the past fifteen years, I've been a member of the Center for Contemporary Printmaking (CCP) in Norwalk, Connecticut. The Center is run by Master Printer Anthony Kirk and offers a wide range of workshops from one or two days up to ten to twelve weeks, and open studio time.

The most memorable workshop I signed up for was by Master Printer Marina Ancona. Since I "discovered" her, I've spent several five-day workshops with her and hope to join her again after I finish writing my memoirs.

In 2005, I had bilateral knee replacement surgery, and I purchased my own press for my home studio when the long trip to Connecticut and six-hour session I spent in the studio there finally became too burdensome. While the press was useful to me and solved the problem of having no convenient alternative, I discovered how lonely the artist's life really was. It is workshops like the many I participated in where artists can emerge from the isolation imposed by the need to create from deep inside and alone. I've missed the opportunity to meet other artists, look at their work, participate in critiques, and to learn!

Reflections

The first ten years of my life in art, I was strictly a painter and was primarily a traditional realist. Over the years, I was told by other artists that working in collage can help bridge the gap from one style to another. When my interest began to evolve toward cubism, I used collage to help smooth that transition.

I did not make a conscious choice to go into cubism or abstract work. For me, it just simply happened as I grew and learned and lived life. What we see and hear is stored in our past and influences what we remember. Whatever we select or are able to recall from our past experience contributes to who we become and, for artists, shapes the direction of their work.

It is said that an artist's twenty-four-hour day consists of one-third creation, one-third management, and the remaining eight hours for sleep! But throughout my art career, there were some highlights that made years of struggle and hard work worthwhile.

The years I worked with Harriet FeBland were very exciting for me. I felt like I discovered new things and progressed every day. Once I was able to devote all my time to art, I could appreciate my progress and become more active in the art world. After so many years during which my art was restricted by more pressing obligations, I felt like a dam broke from inside of me and water spilled everywhere. Not only was I painting every day, but I also became a member of various professional art organizations and participated in group shows. I was determined to contribute to the growth of each group I joined. That and the process of submitting work to juried shows, waiting for positive or negative responses, being rejected and sometimes having work accepted, attending openings, collecting work when the show closed—all this was exciting. But it was time-consuming and sometimes quite draining as well.

The artist begins by showing in local exhibits where submissions are not juried. After a few years, having gained some confidence, the next step is to exhibit in shows where work is selected (and often rejected) by a panel of judges. Once having acquired some experience and success with juried shows, the artist gains insight into various organizations—how they work, what they contribute, what it costs to participate, whether they publicize and how much, what kind of attendance they get at receptions, and the nature of patronage a particular venue will generate.

An artist learns early on that having work rejected is not necessarily a reflection of its quality. But there are times when a jury rejects work that has already won awards, and that can be very frustrating. In spite of such setbacks, it's important for an artist to display his or her work, even though there are pieces the artist might favor and prefer not to sell.

Beginners may fear they will never again paint another work as magnificent as the one just completed. But art only exists when there are viewers who appreciate it. So hiding one's work under the bed or behind a couch when there's no more room in the closet is unacceptable for the artist who seeks a complete sense of accomplishment.

The process of exhibiting and gaining the essential experience can take a very long time. Many shows have their own themes and requirements, which means the preparation and process can be long and difficult for the artist. There were years in my own career where I entered fifteen to twenty juried shows.

The road can be very rocky sometimes. Especially so, since the public at large rarely has any clue how much effort a painting reflects. Nor do they give any thought to what goes on behind the scenes before that painting shows up in the gallery. Just, there it is on the wall, and the viewer likes it or doesn't. Those who like it more often simply enjoy it at the gallery where it is shown. Occasionally, one of these viewers will both like it and be willing and able to purchase it to add to his own art collection.

The crown jewel of art shows is the solo exhibit. A one-person show offers the public a large body of work by a single artist. Maybe even more important, it is often the only occasion when the artist himself can see enough of his own work to consider the span of history it reflects. In the studio, the artist is often working on one piece at a time. Even when I work on two canvases simultaneously, that still reflects just a tiny fraction of my work as an artist and only my most recent self as a painter.

In 1979, after my first solo exhibit was hung, I sat on the floor in the gallery that evening and looked around at my work. Had I really achieved all this? The answer hung there before me.

It was only after my retirement that I could sign up for workshops given during the day and sometimes participate in a two-week workshop. Meantime, I attended several one-week workshops in Vermont at Bennington College. On one occasion, I did so with Harriet FeBland and her Advanced Painters Workshop.

Harriet had lived in London for eleven years when she first married. So it was a very special treat to travel with her to London on one occasion, where we stayed and worked at the Chelsea School of Art, a division of London University. There were seven of us altogether, and we lived in the college dorm in single rooms. Since Harriet knew her way around, she was the perfect guide.

At the Chelsea School of Art in London
Summer, 1985

We all got up early each morning and were first in line for an "English Breakfast" in the college dining hall. From there, we went to the studio where we spent five or six hours each day. In the afternoons, we usually visited museums and galleries or just went sightseeing. We often had tickets for a show or the theater in the evening, or at least went for a fancy dinner. What a memorable time!

My Retrospective Exhibit—2003 (My "Last" Show)

For years—while painting, exhibiting, selling, receiving awards, living with rejection and everything else an artist must endure—I kept looking with a critical eye at each of my finished pieces, imagining the day when it might be selected as part of a retrospective show of my works. Of course, that was little more than a hopeful dream at that point. But what once seems unattainable sometimes does become a reality.

In 2003, the Board of Trustees of Iona College Art Center accepted me for a Solo Show after reviewing my portfolio. Their newly completed Art Center had a beautiful, spacious, well-lit gallery known as the Brother Kenneth Chapman Gallery. That hopeful dream had come true!

"My Long Years' Journey," with forty-four works was curated by two Iona College professors—Stan Lapa and Sheila Kriemelman. The original selection of works to consider was done by Dr. Rosemary Cohane Erpf who also wrote the essay for the Exhibit catalogue. "From Exile into Expression" was the theme of this journey. Dr. Erpf wrote:

> Gerda Roze's Retro celebrates not only a fully developed body of work, but also the triumph of human spirit and creativity against seemingly insurmountable forces. Years later, Roze would recollect this life-determining moment in a large acrylic painting titled "Into Exile," painted more than half a century after the actual escape from communism. The work depicts mother and teenage daughter leaving home and country in 1944 . . .

For this show, ten monotypes were also selected, in which both the technique and the medium are quite different from paintings. For me, monotypes offer a new freedom and possibilities to evolve. There is a spontaneous quality I find adventurous as it becomes visible. Dr. Erpf concludes her essay: "Monotypes serve as visual metaphors for Roze's journey in both her life and her art, which has always been an evolution towards freedom."

My Long Years' Journey
Retrospective Exhibit in 2003
Iona College, Brother Kenneth Chapman Gallery

Two More Solo Shows

I had thought of (and referred to) my 2003 retrospective as "my last show," because I felt, at the time, that it was. I was completely exhausted, depleted of energy, and entirely overworked!

Still, I was rejuvenated by the results, and it was not long before I decided to have yet another exhibit—this time at our Mamaroneck Artists' Guild Gallery located in Larchmont, New York. Each active member who intended to have a show there had to sign up for the next open spot. It usually took three to five years for the opportunity to materialize because artists were accommodated in order of having signed up, and there were a lot of us. But three to five years is just about how long it takes to prepare new works for a solo exhibit! So I went about planning my next show.

The theme I chose was circles, which have fascinated me since way back in Gymnasium where I had been terribly intrigued by geometry. Its focus on points, circles, straight lines, triangles, and planes had a strong grip on my imagination. As I reflected on my earlier works, I began to discover that those concepts were expressed there, however unconsciously. In the more traditional-shaped canvases, the circle emerged as part of the painting, often showing up in my monotypes, and later on taking the form of the canvas itself in many of my constructions.

In preparation for this show, my new works reflected the circular-shaped canvas as a focal part of the painting. While these compositions were essentially abstract, they were often filled with subtly elusive elements and possessed a kind of poetry far beyond formalism.

For my 2010 exhibit of this solo show at MAG Gallery, I engaged a professional curator to select the works and hang the show. I had decided to show a sampling of all my work through the years—paintings, monotypes, and constructions—a total of thirty-two works having, in common, the theme of a circle! The show was entitled "Homage to the Circle."

Thanks to Curator Bruce Kozma who did a superb job by skillfully pulling together all three media and presenting the collection as one unified body, the exhibit was very successful. Five paintings sold! Three of those were purchased by other artists, and that is considered an honor, indeed.

The following year, I was invited by Curator Frank DeGregorie to have a solo show in the "Treasure Room" at the Interchurch Center Galleries in Manhattan. That invitation could not have come at a better time. My home studio was stacked with circle paintings ready to go on exhibit as "Homage to the Circle II."

Ed McCormack, writer, art critic, and publisher of "Gallery and Studio," reviewed my show:

> The tondo or painting in a circular shape was especially popular in Florence, Italy in the fifteenth century. In modern times used only occasionally by painters over the years, this has become sufficiently rare that only one contemporary artist—at least to this writer's knowledge—can be considered its principal exponent: Gerda Roze . . . Indeed, the most important significant difference between Roze's use of the tondo and that of its earlier exponents is that she employs the circular shape for its own sake as a discrete entity integral to her aesthetic intentions rather than a mere vehicle for content.

> Roze's approach to abstraction harks back to the very origins of nonobjective painting as an exploration of the unknown, rather than a calculated formal strategy . . . . One places her very much in the tradition of such early twentieth century, avant-garde pioneers as Kandinsky, Malevich, and Mondrian—to conceive a new language for the unseen while inspired by spiritual systems

of their time . . . . While the spiritual systems that inspired those early masters may have fallen out of favor with the dawning of our scientific age, the human urge to apprehend the unknowable has hardly abated. And it is this that makes the circle, a universal symbol still so pregnant with mystery for every existing culture on the orb that we call the earth, such a rich source of inspiration and innovation for the greatly gifted painter, printmaker and constructionist Gerda Roze.

Whether this show was indeed my last, I don't know. But I have to say, of the eighteen solo shows I have done, it was the best-looking one ever! The gallery itself, with its panels hung from the ceiling, was exceptionally conducive to my works. Each of the seventeen paintings on display was hung on a separate panel. I'm grateful to the talented Curator Frank DeGregorie for his artistic sensitivity in selecting and hanging my works.

"Homage to the Circle II" has become the one to remember.

Diaspora Art Returns—2008

Following the collapse of the Soviet Union in the early 1990s, Latvia became, once again, an independent Democratic Republic. By then, over half a century had elapsed during which hundreds of thousands of Latvian patriots fled the Soviet occupation of their country and settled "temporarily" in the West—the United States, Canada, Australia, Europe, and South America.

We exiles never gave up hope that our country would be free once again and all of us would return. But as months and then years went by, the outlook became bleak. Had it happened within the first five or ten years, a large percentage of us would surely have returned to our homeland. But it was not until U.S. President Ronald Reagan said "Mr. Gorbachev, tear down the Berlin Wall," when events began to pick up speed.

The final outcome felt like it came overnight, but it actually took two generations of hoping and waiting. Young when we emigrated, members of my generation were now in their seventies and eighties with children and grandchildren born in exile by the time the Berlin Wall fell. Consequently, very few of us were in a position to return.

Among the refugees were many artists. Though their homeland had been lost, they created art that reflected their experience, first as displaced persons in Germany, then as immigrants into new countries and even new continents. Artists who left their homelands as small children or who were born during the post-war years today are mature artists. Most of the graduates of the Latvian Academy of Art have passed on. Today's artists of

Latvian descent, educated outside of their homeland, seek relationships with the people and cultural institutions of present-day Latvia.

I did not attend the first two Global Exhibits of All Latvian Art but participated with two of my monotypes. These exhibitions were presented in 1998 at the Latvian National Art Museum "Arsenals" in Riga. We exile artists often tossed around the question of what would happen to our art when we were gone. We wanted to preserve art created by those of us who had left Latvia during the twentieth century Soviet occupation. It seemed to us that we needed to establish in Latvia a center for Latvian Diaspora Art, which would exhibit and preserve a collection of Latvian exile art for future generations.

My painting *Exit* was chosen for our first Diaspora Art Returns Exhibit
Valmiera Museum in Latvia, 2008

Once we conceived of the idea of collecting and preserving art created by artists of Latvian descent outside of Latvia, Lelde Alida Kalmite PhD founded the Global Society of Latvian Art (GSLA). Dr. Kalmite was, herself, a working artist and President of the American Latvian Art Association (ALMA). The GSLA was establishing a center for Latvian Diaspora Art in Latvia. It was a tremendous undertaking. But with the help of a committee created from the ALMA membership, the project took off.

In the autumn of 2008, a two-month exhibit of contemporary art by exile Latvian artists from all over the globe was organized, and close to a hundred works were shipped, including mine. The requirement for participation was to submit three images to a jury and to have one piece selected for the exhibit. My painting they chose was entitled *Exit*. It was not the one I would have picked, but the jury has the last word. This painting was a large acrylic, horizontal diptych depicting a male figure departing into the fog. The palette was tones of pale blue and green, with some pink to purple shades—all kept to a somber mood.

VII

My Friend Josephine

One Saturday morning in Spring of 1978, I had a golf date with my friend Louise. Neither of us was a good golfer. Not even close! I was a frank beginner, determined to give golf a chance and see if the game was for me.

My friends had tried to convince me. "Golf is a great game! You'll be walking—always outdoors—and you'll meet nice people." What they neglected to bring to my attention is how expensive a game it actually is. It could easily cost seventy bucks for a Saturday game at a local public golf course. This was way too steep for my budget. But I scrimped on other things and somehow made it all work.

Louise and I drove out to Banksville, a small community on the Connecticut-New York border. I'd never been there, but Louise liked it because it was never crowded, so there was no waiting time and we could tee off immediately.

When we arrived, there was a woman waiting alone to tee off just ahead of us. I knew Louise preferred to play as a twosome, but I asked if she minded inviting the lady to join us and make it a threesome. Louise agreed, and that's how I met Josephine Nord who remained my good friend for twenty-five years until her death in 2003.

What brought us together and nurtured our long-lasting friendship was our love for the game that we pursued only on weekends. Two or three times during the summer Jo and I would go away for a weekend to a resort hotel that offered a golf weekend special—usually to upstate New York or to the New Jersey shore. There, we could play to our hearts' desire, sometimes thirty-six holes in one day!

When I first met Jo, she worked for a large fashion conglomerate in Midtown Manhattan. She was executive secretary to the company's president. Jo was very fashion conscious and wore gorgeous clothes. She was tall and slim, with beautiful, naturally blonde hair. Everything looked good on her!

Unlike me, Jo was a very private person. Only occasionally would she speak of her family and past. It took many golf games and stopovers at the

"Nineteenth Hole" for a tuna sandwich and Miller's Light before I learned more of her past.

Josephine Nord, nee Trebuth, was born in Manhattan in 1931, the youngest of five daughters, to German immigrant parents. Her father was a day laborer and never earned much money. Her mother, also named Josephine, held the family together and ran a boarding house in Yorkville, a section of Manhattan that was heavily populated by German immigrants following WWI.

The boarding house was hard work, but this provided the family with a meager income. As children, Jo and her sisters helped their mother clean the rooms, do the laundry, and cook meals. It was a daily struggle for survival. All the girls went to school during the week, and on Sundays, the family attended a Lutheran church.

Jo grew up with a very strong sense of family responsibility. She graduated from Julia Richmond High School in Manhattan and later attended Hunter College. In the late sixties, she married—the only sister to do so. For the first time in her life, she moved away from her family and lived with her husband in California.

When she and I first met, Jo had just returned from California, following the burial of her husband who succumbed to a five-year struggle with cancer. He had been diagnosed even before the honeymoon began. "Our honeymoon was spent going to doctors and hospitals," she told me. "But he was a wonderful person, and I loved him so much that nothing felt too difficult for me. I lived day to day and hoped for a miracle."

Jo had already had the experience of taking care of her father for many years following a stroke he suffered before he retired. At first, he was home; but later, he was confined to a nursing facility. A younger sister Edith was born with Down's syndrome, though she would live past her sixtieth birthday. Edith was the darling and sunshine of the whole Trebuth family.

Jo's mother lived a long life and continued to be the stronghold and support for the family, taking care of her invalid husband for years, as well as her beloved Edith. When Jo's mother passed on, Edith required full-time care. The oldest sister, Gertrude, had passed away from cancer when she was in her forties. That left Jo and sisters Julia and Anna to take care of Edith.

Anna was not very ambitious by nature and lived for the day rather than striving to succeed or do better in life. So it was decided that she should retire from her menial job and remain at home to care for Edith.

By the time I met the sisters, it was Jo and Julia who were primarily running the show. Julia had an impressive business career, having reached the top of the corporate ladder. She was CEO/treasurer of a large chemical corporation. So she took care of the family finances while Jo was the business manager.

Jo and Julia, of the five sisters, had the closest relationship. Even so, they were very different in nature and temperament. Julia was soft-spoken and dealt with family crises in a calm and mature manner. Jo, on the other hand, could be explosive and verbose. But somehow their personalities complemented each other and, together, they got things done.

Josephine Nord with her sister Julia Trebuth

In time, when Jo and I met for a golf date, I began to notice she had trouble concentrating on the game. I asked her how things were at home, and she simply said, "The arrangement with Anna caring for Edith just is not working out."

Upon Jo's return from California, she and sister Julia had purchased a beautiful three-bedroom condo in Hartsdale where Jo shared a bedroom with Edith, and Julia and Anna shared one. Now, Edith had contracted cancer and required special care. Anna was not willing or able to do more than she already had done, and the sisters began to disagree and to fight.

So Anna, now in her seventies, decided to move out and start life all over again. Her friends had encouraged her independence albeit Anna's first such experience, and they found a small apartment for her in New Rochelle. Across the street was the United Hebrew Home for the Aged where Anna said she could buy her meals. But the meal tickets from the nursing home never materialized, and soon Anna was in financial trouble.

Julia had set up a Government Savings Bond account for Anna some years before, from which Julia now began to withdraw money by selling one bond at a time to supply Anna with financial assistance. There were days when Jo was distraught over Anna's determination to free herself from her family. But Jo and Julia stood by her in spite of the growing burden.

Meanwhile, Edith's condition grew worse, and she had to be fed through a tube. Jo took over this responsibility and, for the next two years until Edith's death, Jo insisted upon returning home by 6:00 p.m. sharp to feed and take care of her sister. Finally, Julia decided to retire and stay home herself. It was a very difficult time.

One day, the New Rochelle Hospital called to inform Anna Trebuth's family that Anna had fallen on ice and her back was broken. After back surgery, a long stay in the hospital, and months of physical therapy, Anna was ready to be released to a nursing facility where she remained bedridden for eleven long years until her death in 2006.

Once Anna had settled into the nursing home, there were decisions to be made about the cost of her care, her personal debts, and who was going to be responsible. Jo handled all the red tape for Medicaid once all Anna's personal assets were spent. At that point, Anna's Social Security check, a small pension from her former employer and the remainder of her U.S. Savings Bond account went straight to the nursing home. She had a monthly allowance of fifty dollars for incidentals. Julia and Jo deposited supplemental money into her nursing home Special Needs Account and looked after Anna's welfare to make sure she had whatever she needed or wanted.

Meanwhile, in addition to Jo's struggles with her family, the company she worked for moved back to Chicago and had plans to close their New York office. The choice to move or lose her job could not have come at a more inopportune time. So at the age of sixty-seven, she became unemployed, having decided to stay in New York. While collecting unemployment benefits, Jo vigorously looked for a full-time job. This wasn't just difficult. At her age, it was virtually impossible.

She had to settle for part-time jobs or sometimes temporary assignments. I tried to encourage her to believe that she simply had to be patient—that something would come along. But patience was not among Jo's many virtues. Even so, almost a year later, Jo was hired by a communications company in Stamford.

After Edith passed on and Anna was settled into the nursing home, there followed a short period of time where Julia and Jo had no emergencies or sleepless nights. But that was not meant to last. In 1999, Julia, too, died of cancer, leaving a substantial estate to Jo and naming her as executrix.

Although Jo and I were good friends and had enjoyed each other's company for so many years, there was always a line beyond which Jo rarely ventured into her personal past. She never said how substantial an estate she'd inherited from Julia. Only that the inheritance tax was quite burdensome. Jo had a friend from her youth named Loretta who probably served as her confidante. But with me, Jo could be very secretive.

"I don't know, Gerda," she said to me once, "how you can manage everything with your income. You must have a secret formula."

I had always tried to live debt-free, except for the mortgage, the car, and the baby grand. True, this wasn't easy, but I never missed a payment. Often I hid what I considered my own private struggle behind a shiny exterior. For years, I bought designer clothes in thrift shops, and I still own several nice pieces of furniture purchased at the Salvation Army. I was never ashamed of any of this. It just didn't seem to be relevant to casual conversation. I knew who I was and where I came from.

Once I retired, I had a pretty rough time between mortgage payments and coop maintenance on an income reduced by half. But I offered Jo my help from time to time, which she rarely accepted. She was very independent and preferred to take care of her family herself. This was one area in which she and I were quite similar, and I understood her determination. I imagine this probably comes from the lifelong necessity to stand on your own two feet in order to accomplish anything.

Soon after Julia's demise, Jo seemed to have more frequent doctors' appointments. One day she asked me to drive her to the Columbia-Presbyterian Hospital in Manhattan for a consultation with a well-known breast cancer surgeon. Soon thereafter, she underwent surgery but did not follow the surgeon's advice to have a radical mastectomy. Instead, she chose the newly developed method of removing cancerous lymph nodes without removing her breasts. The surgery was successful, and she went back to work. For a while.

Then, I was hit by a car while crossing the street. I suffered a slight brain concussion, broken nose, and had stitches around my mouth and lips. My arthritis had also begun to affect my spine by this time. By the following spring, I still wasn't in very good shape to get back on the golf course. So Jo joined the Lake Isle Club, which gave her more freedom to tee off practically whenever she wanted without fighting crowds and long waits at each hole. I couldn't afford the membership fee, anyway, and my golf dates with Jo became irregular and less frequent. Oh, how I missed the game! But life went on.

Late in 2002, about two years after breast surgery, Jo was seeing the oncologist again. This time it was her esophagus. First an inflammation, which turned out to be cancerous. I could see it was very serious this time. Now, on occasion, she would accept my offer to help her in some way. Still, she would often say, "There will be plenty of times when you'll have to help me. Save it now, Gerda, until I ask for it. As long as I can do it myself, that's what I will do." Jo was a fighter! Christmas Eve she insisted upon driving me to Scarsdale to attend her church—the Hitchcock Presbyterian.

Since my retirement from consulting in 1987, I had worked for H&R Block seventeen seasons, five years of which I worked for LaPorta & LaPorta's Law Firm. I worked full time during tax season and couldn't take Jo to her doctors.

"I don't understand why you continue to work for H&R Block," Jo told me. "You deal with a horrible clientele in the Bronx and make hardly any money at all!"

There was some truth to what Jo said, but I loved working with all kinds of people as I experienced every tax season. I had met the most honest, decent, and hardworking folks right down to "professional" crooks. I remember joking with my coworkers at Block that I would write a book when I retired about my life as a tax preparer. That book, of course, never materialized. But even beyond the interesting people I met, I was also especially gratified to have reached the level of senior tax advisor. Besides that, the six to nine thousand dollars I earned for the season covered my annual art expenses.

Once Jo came to accept the seriousness of her illness, she geared into organizing her entire life. Just in case anything happened. Then came the news that her lifelong friend Loretta had suffered a massive stroke. It was Loretta whom Jo had designated to be executrix of her will and administrator of her estate. She knew Loretta would follow her detailed instructions, and now Loretta, while still alive, could not speak or move! Jo became frantic.

Finally, she asked if I would be willing to handle it. I was really taken aback. By then, after all, I was seventy-seven and felt she should find a younger person. When she explained to me that she'd already approached two such friends who had both declined, I felt I needed to say yes. I sensed Jo's time was running out.

She decided to use my lawyer, as well, and that was a great relief to me, since I knew he would help guide me through the process. I drove Jo to my lawyer as she asked me to do and sat in the waiting room while she met with him. I knew she was changing Loretta's name to mine as executrix. And I knew she wanted to make me Anna's primary caretaker and have me visit Anna in the nursing home to make sure her needs were fulfilled.

Then, I was asked to sign all the necessary papers. I had no idea what I was getting into. I declined the administrator's commission, stating that I intended to carry out this role from my friendship with Jo. But she insisted I agree to accept it. As she put it then, "You better agree to the commission, Gerda, because you will earn it. I want you to work very hard for every dime I'm leaving to you."

The last three months of her life, I spent more and more time with her. When it became necessary to arrange for hospice care to come into her home, I became her primary caretaker. That became a full-time job for me, and I practically moved in with her. I had to ensure that she had twenty-four-hour care, and I couldn't do this alone. One of my biggest frustrations was that I could never depend on the Home Healthcare people despite the generous hourly rate we paid for the privilege. Jo had always been very careful with her money, so I struggled to manage the expenses involved in order to keep them reasonable. But it wasn't easy.

At first I tried to stay with Jo nights and have help come during the day. Her friends tried to help whenever I asked and would get things from the store, pick up medication, or stay with Jo if I had to go home for a few hours.

But cancer of the esophagus is a very nasty type of cancer. The pain concentrates in the throat, chest, and down into the stomach. Gradually, it affects breathing and swallowing, and produces a constant dry cough. Jo suffered terribly. Toward the end, she could hardly swallow at all and had to live on liquids alone.

Gradually, I began to realize the responsibilities were taking their toll on me. Jo and I got along very well, and I knew she appreciated all that I did. But there was one incident where Jo became very angry with me over something I must have said or misunderstood.

"Do I have to get a translator to make you understand me?" she yelled.

I was extremely upset, even angry. But I walked into the kitchen, made myself a cup of coffee, sat down to dry my tears, and calm myself by thinking about all that had transpired in my life. To think about Jo and her needs and how good a friend she had been. To imagine what else I could do for her and whether I was up to the task. I had to find a better way to handle the responsibilities Jo had entrusted me with. "I want you all to work hard for every nickel I'm leaving you . . ." That's what she'd said and I was beginning to understand what she meant.

In 2003, Jo died in my arms. The estate she left was very large. One-third of that estate was willed to Jo's friend Loretta, a permanent nursing home resident by now. Another third went to other friends and charities. And one-third was left to me.

I had never imagined the size of Jo's estate. She and I had never discussed her income or assets or even her salary. Even when the lawyer read Jo's will, I did not grasp its implications. He gave me a copy to take home and read, which I did. Then, it began to sink in.

Jo and I had often talked about nursing homes and our shared view of the atmosphere in those we were familiar with. We both felt the option of dying at home in familiar surroundings was, when that was possible, far preferable to the finality one could sense in a nursing home environment.

Of course, we had both had some considerable experience with nursing homes where various family members had gone—Jo's father and sister Anna; my own Uncle Arthur. Neither of us thought nursing homes were anything to look forward to. During the time I took care of Jo, she said to me, "I want to make sure you never have to go into a nursing home."

Now, I realized that was not just a wish on Jo's part but her very clear intention.

Following Jo's death in 2003, I became Anna's official caretaker until she passed away in 2006. According to detailed instructions left for me by Jo, I also made sure Anna was well treated by the staff and that her Special Needs Account never fell below two hundred dollars.

For my own part and for the first time in my life, I no longer had to struggle to pay every bill, which was a great relief. Every day, something reminds me of Jo, and all I can say is just, "Thank you."

As long as I can still visit the cemetery, I will place a dozen of Jo's favorite blush-colored roses on the marble floor in front of her crypt.

VIII

My Son Olaf

On April 18, 1951, my son Olaf was delivered by cesarean section at the Lutheran Hospital in Manhattan on Convent Avenue in Harlem. Based on my financial situation and circumstance, I did not pay for anything. That was the first and last time in my life I was considered to be a welfare case.

The hospital ward was a large room with ten beds, mine being bed number eight. As far as I know, there was no such thing there as a semi-private room, but the maternity ward was a happy place where the biggest event in one's life came to pass. Visiting hours were full of excitement, where proud fathers beamed, having done what I felt was less than their share of the work. They'd march in with flowers and candy, kiss their wives and hug their new babies.

I knew my mother and Arthur would come, but only late in the night. How I envied the others their candy and flowers . . . and babies' fathers. Finally, my mother and Arthur arrived. My mother brought me a dozen, long-stemmed American Beauties, and Uncle Arthur bought me a beautiful gold bracelet to celebrate the occasion. Mother was completely composed during the entire event. But Uncle Arthur was positively delirious! He kept repeating "It's a boy! It's a boy!" as if I'd performed a miracle.

Still, I wanted to tell everyone in the ward that I actually did have a husband. It was 1951, after all, and being a single mom was not very highly regarded. There was a nurse on the ward who came in every morning and went bed to bed massaging our breasts. One day, when she finished with me, she turned to the other mothers and announced in a pretty loud voice: "Women, may I have your attention. I want you to see what perfect breasts look like after giving birth. Mrs. Dobrzanski has perfect breasts. After all these years in nursing, I've never seen anything so beautiful."

I was mortified. But that put a damper on any rumors and gave Mrs. Dobrzanski's morale the boost that it needed.

Mrs. Treiber, a warmhearted lady I'd met at church, brought me and Olaf home from the hospital. All I had for the baby were a package of diapers, a shirt, and a little cap my mother had made for him. I placed Olaf into a drawer I pulled from my dresser. Soon after that, generous people began giving me baby clothes, carriages, even a crib—all the things babies need and outgrow. I couldn't believe it!

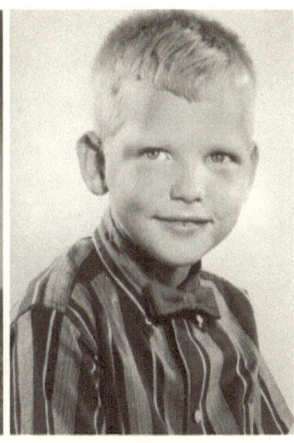

The traditional sailor suit   Olaf on his sixth birthday
was a must for every boy.   in 1957
Olaf, age 2 ½

Beginning in Olaf's early childhood when he was only six, I would take him to Monroe High School every Saturday morning for swimming lessons. The school was located in the Bronx near where we lived at that time. He loved going and worked hard, hoping to receive a swimming scholarship for college, but that never materialized. He was, as they say, a big fish in his high school Swim Pond. But even a big fish could not compete with swimmers who participated in the Olympics while still in high school. Olaf's grades were on a medium level, though I was always convinced he could do better with a little more effort. And I often pushed him to improve.

Olaf graduated from Mount Vernon High School in 1970

When Olaf and I began to look for a college, his ideas differed from mine. His main objective was a school with a great swim team. Mine, on the other hand, was a school with an abundance of PhDs on the teaching staff. Luckily, we found a compromise that appeared to offer both—Colorado State University.

Throughout his college years, Olaf coached Westchester County swim teams. He loved working with the young swimmers and they adored him. These summers may have been the happiest of his life!

The day Olaf left for college in Colorado, he told me he wanted to meet his father and asked for my help. He and I agreed not to mention this to Grandma who was quite ill by that time, fighting cancer. I gave him the information I had, though I certainly hadn't kept track of Klemens or his whereabouts over the years. I urged Olaf to look up his father's telephone number in Pittsburgh and give him a call. By having him speak to his father first before meeting him, I hoped to save Olaf from any disappointment he might face otherwise.

Instead, Olaf went directly to his father's home where Klemens—physically and emotionally—embraced his lost son. When Olaf returned, he told me how wonderful his father had been. Olaf had found in Klemens a new home and new family, having also acquired two brothers and two sisters! So Klemens was now married, and his oldest daughter was a year or two younger than Olaf. Klemens was now a foreman in a steel mill, and Olaf was very proud of his father.

For the first time in my life, I became hysterical. I cried and could not stop. I wasn't prepared for Klemens to resurface in his son's life so suddenly, nor for that to be such an immediately happy experience for Olaf. The nineteen intervening years had been exhausting and difficult ones. Yes, I was happy for Olaf that he finally had a meaningful relationship with his father. But in sharp contrast, everything I'd experienced myself flooded back in that moment. Olaf had never seen me in such a state, and I'm sure he was shocked.

From that point on, Olaf kept in contact with his father and family, visiting them regularly when travelling to and from Colorado. Once he finished school, he and his young bride Koren would visit with them from their own home in Wyoming.

After his first semester at CSU, he returned for Christmas to tell me he did not intend to go back to school there. He had not made the college swim team, and his grades were not the best either. The news wasn't the greatest of Christmas gifts, but I have always believed deeply that things work out for the best because Someone is watching over us and leading us by His hand.

For the preceding five years, Mother's health had gradually deteriorated, and she lived in pain most of the time. No doctor had managed to come up with a diagnosis. Finally, she became bedridden, and I had to agree to "exploratory" surgery. As she waited for admission to the hospital, she required help during the day. Since I had to work and could not be there all day, Olaf and I came up with a plan. He would enroll in the local Westchester Community College where he would attend night classes, so he could take care of his beloved "Omi" during the day.

Mother had taken care of Olaf since he was six weeks old. She had always been strict with him but still fair and loving. Asian cultures sometimes refer to the mothers and grandmothers in extended families as "Mother Number One" and "Mother Number Two." In my case, "Mother Number One" to Olaf was my own mother, and I was most certainly "Number Two." My role was that of a friend, confidante, sister, and pal. But it was Omi who had the authority.

Olaf loved her dearly. How much devotion he displayed when caring for her in the last months of her life! In May 1971, Mother died of cancer at the age of seventy-five. After the funeral, Olaf returned to Colorado to a small college in Trinidad, which borders New Mexico. He had decided to major in forestry.

Olaf was still in his first semester at Trinidad College when he saw a small ad posted on the board in the student hall. "Clean-cut young man with driver's license may apply for a part-time job as a limo driver for a funeral home. Pay set at $2/hour." Olaf did not waste a minute. He shaved, put on a clean shirt and tie, and off he went to apply for the job and was hired on the spot by the owner.

Olaf knew we did not have much money, but one way or another we always had managed. I urged him to concentrate on his studies at school and forget about finding a part-time job. Finally, although it was against my own better judgment, I agreed to this job at the funeral home when Olaf assured me his work hours would not interfere with his classes.

The owner, Mr. B, was an older gentleman—a wealthy self-made man with mortuary school certifications. He and his staff were very nice people as Olaf often reported. Two of the younger morticians had college degrees. Mr. B was born and grew up in the same town, having spent his childhood on "the other side of the tracks" where he was raised by his mother. At age twelve, he went to work to help out his family and got a job working for a local doctor.

By now, Mr. B was in his late sixties, married, father of two grown daughters, and had several grandchildren. He was well liked in the community and was known for his charitable nature. From time to time, Olaf would tell me what a nice guy Mr. B was and how good he and his wife were, especially to young people. They would take in runaways, feed and clothe them, and sometimes pay their college tuition. The community surrounding the funeral home was relatively poor, and the Bs were known for their generosity, sometimes donating their funeral services to those with no means to pay.

Olaf was very fond of Mr. B who treated him like a son, and eventually, Mr. B offered Olaf a room in the funeral home where he could mind their twenty-four-hour telephone line. Olaf recognized this as an opportunity to save himself the cost he now paid for a shared college dormitory room. I spoke with Mr. or Mrs. B on occasion, asking about my son. They assured me they all loved him and that he was doing a very good job. Often they would invite me to come for a visit.

In the summer of 1974, I flew to Denver and rented a car there to drive the two hours down to Trinidad. My plan was to cross the Rockies after my visit and take Olaf with me so we could spend some time on the West Coast. The stay with my son was great. He even agreed to come with me across the Rockies to the West Slope. Mr. and Mrs. B treated me royally.

The night before leaving Trinidad, Olaf suddenly changed his mind and decided he had to rush off to New York. Mrs. B asked if I could give her a ride to a nearby town where their daughter lived, and I was glad to accommodate. The next morning, she and I left early, just as the fog from the valley began to lift, leaving a blanket of water droplets behind. The air was crisp, and I turned on my heater. There was hardly any traffic on this leisurely morning and the time flew by as we chatted about this and that. Soon, our conversation turned to her husband when I expressed my admiration for his caring heart.

It seems the two had married young, and it was only after their first child was born that Mrs. B began to have misgivings about her husband and their relationship. Mr. B made frequent trips to Denver, which Mrs. B referred to facetiously as "business trips." Though her husband denied it, Mrs. B began to suspect that he was homosexual. In the small town where they lived, everyone knew everyone else, which made it hard to keep family secrets. Being a good, practicing Catholic, Mrs. B stifled her suspicions and hoped some miracle would save their marriage and keep her family intact.

After the birth of their second daughter, Mr. B began to attract young homeless boys by offering them a temporary place to live, and her marriage began to fall apart. "I tried," said Mrs. B, "to fight for my place in our marriage. But who were my adversaries? Young kids. Boys as young as twelve or thirteen." Even Mrs. B's priest suggested a divorce as the best and only solution. But she felt she had invested too much into her marriage to give it all up. Was it possible that the accumulated wealth she shared with her husband was all that kept the two bound together?

As I drove and listened, I began to feel like a dark cloud was closing in on me and any moment lightning would strike. Stories Olaf had told me about the other young boys who worked at the funeral home began to recast themselves in a shadowy light, and Mrs. B's story started to sound distant. Tears blurred my vision, and my whole body began to shake. I could not drive any longer. I had to inhale the cool, fresh mountain air and collect myself. So I stopped at a diner for a cup of coffee.

Now came my burning question to Mrs. B. "What about my son?"

"Olaf," she said, "did not submit himself to my husband." She swore on the Bible that this was the truth. I was emotionally drained, having arrived at the very brink of a revelation I was not prepared to accept. Thank you, Lord!

I parted company with Mrs. B when I dropped her off at her daughter's house and continued my trip. I no longer felt like sightseeing, but maybe I wasn't yet ready to go home either. What little I do remember from the remainder of my trip was considerably blurred by the uncomfortable discussion Mrs. B and I had though I cannot forget the harrowing experience of driving across the Rocky Mountains.

I had not realized that crossing the Rockies alone in a car was taking a very big risk. No one had warned me. One moment I'd be driving through a meadow with blooming field flowers, and the next it would begin to snow, turning the road into a slippery bed of ice.

At one point, my car stalled and began to slide backward. I shifted into reverse and tried to maneuver slightly off the center of the road, hoping the car would just stop. It did, and I took a deep breath. Although I was safe for the moment, I resented the fact that Olaf had not come along as we had originally planned. It seemed to me very thoughtless of him to allow me to cross the mountains alone. I did reach Mesa Verde on the West slope, and I toured the prehistoric cliff dwellings on my way through Colorado Springs to Denver Airport.

I was still preoccupied with Mrs. B's story about her husband. I realized I had sometimes wondered if Olaf's perception of him was just too good to be true. By then, the sexual revolution had begun to unfold, but little was discussed openly about matters of sexuality. Call me naive or even stupid. Truth was I'd had no specific misgivings as long as my son assured me everything was okay. But that experience in the summer that year affected me deeply.

By the time I returned to New York, I was ready to talk to Olaf.

"I have learned all there is to know about Mr. B from his wife," I told him. "Now, I want to hear it from you. What happened?"

Olaf paused for a minute. "There are things I did not tell you about Mr. B because I did not want to upset you," he said. "But be assured that I never got involved in any of his activities. I have done nothing wrong. He never touched me or proposed anything I would regard as improper. He always treated me with respect. He was like a father to me, and I treasure his trust in me."

He continued: "For quite a while, I did not suspect anything wrong going on in the funeral home. The kids he hired, I truly believed, were boys he rescued from worse environments so he could be helpful to them. Our chores and pay were usually similar. But there was one boy who seemed to get away with murder, and that annoyed the heck out of me because I ended up doing his work."

As Olaf related this story to me, I remembered we had spoken about this kid and that Mr. B had promised them both a vacation trip to Denver. "Denver!" Suddenly, the circumstances surrounding that trip gave me an ominous feeling.

Olaf went on to report that the big day finally arrived, and the three of them set off for Denver. Mr. B rented one room with two double beds and took them to a show, a gay bar, and to dinner. They had a good time, but some things had bothered Olaf—especially what he saw going on in the gay bar.

It was early morning by the time they returned to their hotel room. Mr. B picked one bed and pointed to the other for Olaf. Olaf had expected a folding bed to be set up in the room for the third guest, but there was none. So he climbed into the bed Mr. B indicated for him. Once the lights went out, the kid crawled in with Olaf!

"Oh no! Not in my bed," he cried out. "If you want to sleep in my bed, go ahead. I'll sleep on the floor." And that's what he did. End of story.

At the beginning of Olaf's senior year, he informed me that he planned to switch his major and go into mortuary science. There were only three colleges in the whole country offering degrees in Mortuary Science, and he had picked Southern Illinois University (SIU) in Carbondale.

Mortuary science? I thought. I tried to be fair in my judgment, but that took some time to sink in. We all die, of course, and someone must care for our bodies. But my own dreams for Olaf had not included this possibility. When he was a child, I had imagined him as a West Point graduate with a military career, just like his father and his grandfather before him. When it became evident that would not work out, and with my mother's help, I had begun to see him as a wildlife conservationist or forest ranger. "Not much money in it," Mami would say, "but a healthy and happy life."

But a funeral director? If Grandma were still alive, she would have "straightened him out" as had been her role. But me? Of course, I went along. There was no time to waste, I thought. I checked out the curriculum for a mortuary science program, and what I learned sounded promising. The coursework covered science, business administration, and psychology—family and funeral. It seemed to have potential—a solid background for any job, really.

Finally, in 1976, having switched schools and majors multiple times, Olaf was ready to graduate from SIU with a degree in mortuary science.

Olaf met Koren Shisler while both were students at SIU. She was an arts major. From time to time, he would mention having met a very nice girl from the Midwest. Eventually, they began dating. Soon after that, he announced to me that they had decided to marry following graduation. I had planned to attend my son's graduation, of course, but now I had two celebrations to consider!

My best and oldest girlfriend in this country was Eleanor Diviaczky. She wanted to join me. She had watched Olaf grow up, and she cared for him a great deal, having never married or had children herself. I was so grateful to Eleanor for wanting to accompany me. Graduation was one thing, but now we were dealing with Olaf's wedding, and I knew she would be my ally.

Eleanor had never met Klemens in person, but she often expressed her distaste for "that man," as she called him. It was incomprehensible to her that a man would not ask for visiting rights to see his own son and never seemed to have any desire to get to know his own flesh and blood.

Graduation was to take place in Carbondale. The wedding would be two days later in Pekin, a small suburb of Peoria, Illinois. Because of the distance between New York and Illinois, everything had to be planned and scheduled over the phone. And time was of the essence.

Immediately, I made reservations for a flight to Peoria to meet with the bride's parents, thinking it would be appropriate to be introduced to Koren's mother and father before the Big Day. God forbid I should have to meet them outside the church five minutes before the ceremony, which just didn't seem proper to me. And I must admit, before anything else, I had to become familiar with wedding etiquette here in the States.

I began to read up on wedding rules and discovered that Amy Vanderbilt's acknowledged expertise is quite comprehensive. Among other things, I learned I was responsible for a rehearsal dinner, customarily given by the groom's parents. The least problem, so I thought, would be to find the proper restaurant since Koren's parents were locals after all.

For my trip to Peoria, I had a twofold mission: to meet the bride and her parents, and to discuss some of the details of the planned wedding. My burning concern surrounded the receiving line at the reception. Olaf had told them his parents were divorced, but I wondered if standing alone on one side of the newlyweds while the bride's parents stood together on the other would be all right. They thought that was fine. I asked Koren's mother what she planned to wear to the afternoon wedding—long dress or short? What color? After all, I wanted to accommodate the wishes of the mother of the bride. But to all my questions, she would just smile and say, "Whatever you wish is fine with me."

In the few hours I had to spend with Koren's family, we didn't even get to my questions about a suitable restaurant for dinner after the rehearsal. I had hoped for a separate room for an intimate dinner party. But some days later, Koren's mother called to tell me about a "nice family restaurant" she thought would accommodate the rehearsal dinner. They did not have private dining rooms, so the party would be seated at a table for twelve and could "squeeze in" another chair, if we needed.

That didn't seem exactly right to me though. So I called the banquet manager at the Hilton Hotel in Peoria and made a reservation for fifteen guests. I specified in great detail what I wanted—a private room with two waiters and a chef, among other things.

Olaf and I broached the sticky subject of who should be invited to this dinner. He, of course, wanted his father and his father's entire family. The lovely, intimate dinner party I envisioned, on the other hand, had not included them. But Olaf was insistent on this point, and I conceded at least that his father could come, but certainly not the whole family. That was unacceptable to Olaf.

"Have it your way," I finally said. "Let your father give this dinner party, and I will stay out of it. I'll come to your wedding and skip the rehearsal dinner myself."

This must have put Olaf on the spot, and he said that was out of the question because he wanted me there too. One of us had to compromise, and this time it was Olaf. His father was not invited.

The final package delivered by the Hilton was exquisite. The private dining room was decorated in white and blue with flowers and beautiful chandeliers. Suffice it to say that the dinner party turned out to be the most elegant I'd ever given!

As the wedding day approached, I got very nervous and stressed out. How would I face Klemens after an entire quarter century? Here I was fifty-one years old, and my twenty-five-year-old son was getting married. I had left my husband a long time before and had chosen a single life. I had accomplished a lot during those years. I had finished my education, established myself as a professional in the corporate world, and taken care of my family. Even so, I was lonely. Twice, I had even wished I had a husband on my side—once in the hospital when my son was born, and now as I contemplated being walked down the aisle escorted by an usher. I felt like I'd never healed from having been wounded so many years before. And now, I felt incomplete.

Olaf married Koren Shisler in Pekin, Illinois in 1976

An elderly Lutheran pastor had arranged the church seating after Olaf explained that his parents were divorced. "Tell me, who brought you up and took care of you?" the pastor asked.

"My mother," said Olaf, to which the pastor declared, "Your mother will be seated in the first pew; the next will be left empty. In the third will be seated your father and his family."

The final hurdle was to decide who was to stand in the receiving line. Although Koren's parents and I had discussed the receiving line on my visit to Peoria, Olaf apparently had another plan in mind. I had to remind myself it was his wedding, not mine. Klemens kept a very low profile throughout my obvious "negotiations" with Olaf. Finally, I walked over to him and asked him to join me in the receiving line. "After all," I said, "it is our son's wedding day."

The reception was given by Koren's parents in a beautiful country club setting. There were over a hundred invited guests. Most of them represented the bride's side of the family, along with a handful of Olaf's college pals.

As Eleanor and I drove into the country club parking lot for the wedding reception, Klemens, too, arrived with his family. All I could think of was, "Remember, this is your son's wedding. Put aside all your personal feelings." Eleanor and I approached Klemens and were introduced to his wife and two of his children. I shook hands with Klemens, and he held on to mine with both of his hands and said, "I had a long time to think everything over, and I know now I made many mistakes. I hope you can forgive me."

I don't remember responding.

I didn't know how many of the guests were aware Olaf's parents were divorced and that his father was with his present wife Joan and their children. Up to this point, I had kept my married name so Olaf could avoid unnecessary explanations while growing up. I would change it back to my maiden name following his graduation and wedding. But now, his father and I were introduced as Mr. and Mrs. Dobrzanski—the right and proper way. I had duly fulfilled my son's wishes.

As the party began to break up and we all said our good-byes, Klemens came to me and said, "Gerda, I want to thank you for having brought up our son, such a fine young man. I owe you a sincere thank you." And with that, he kissed my hand.

These words from Klemens brought closure to my long struggle to turn my life's painful disappointments into forgiveness. I had found peace. For the next few years, Olaf kept in contact with his father and their family until Klemens was diagnosed with Alzheimer's disease and gradually slid into a faraway place.

After Olaf married in August of 1976, he and Koren settled in Denver where he got a funeral director position and Koren worked for a credit company. Three months later, in November, my company sent me on a business trip to Denver. What good fortune to visit the newlyweds! I was very excited and looked forward to spending a weekend with them. I also sensed a similar excitement and maybe some nervousness in Koren.

We hardly knew each other and had met only three previous times, one of which was their wedding. Besides, Koren was only nineteen, and I'm sure she wanted to put her best foot forward to impress her new mother-in-law.

They lived in a two-bedroom apartment and had managed to furnish it in a short time, though barely. I thought that was very admirable. I slept in the second bedroom and even had fresh flowers on my night table. I have to admit the naughty thought crossed my mind that these flowers might have come from the funeral home.

The first night, we stayed in, since Koren had planned to serve up a fried chicken dinner. After dinner, we spent hours talking. There was so much to catch up on—their recent graduation, the wedding, and their new jobs.

Olaf loved the West. Born and raised in New York, he never really enjoyed City life. Something always drew him to the country. Once he left for Colorado State University, he rarely came back East except for an occasional visit. During his college years, he'd return to Westchester and find a summer job back home, working as a lifeguard to save money for school.

It was really no wonder he settled first in Colorado following college and later moving to Wyoming. I never understood how a boy from New York could give up all the big city offers to live way out in the sticks. But he seemed very happy to be there, and his happiness was my main concern.

He loved what he was doing and where he was living. Money was not everything, in his view. When I asked him what he liked about his work, his answer was simple. "Dealing with grieving families is my greatest satisfaction. To be able to speak with them and help them through their difficult hours is very rewarding. To stand by them and support them with compassion and understanding." That was my son, the idealist.

At one point that evening, Koren went into the kitchen and then asked Olaf to take out the trash. She might have even asked twice. Next morning, I was up first and went into the kitchen to make coffee, and there sat the trash bag, still waiting for Olaf to remove it.

"Good morning, Mom!" he said from the doorway. "And how did you sleep?"

"Take out this garbage right now!" I responded. End of conversation.

The second night, I took them to Denver's famous Bank Deposit Restaurant for dinner. When we returned home, I sensed something was not right, and soon a big fight broke out with crying and tears. Koren grabbed her pocketbook, said she was leaving, and ran out the door.

There I sat—an outsider, and a guest to boot—in the midst of a family quarrel. All I could think of was, *My goodness, what's happening? They're only three months married. Did I cause this in some way? Or was it the trash bag incident from last night and this morning?* Truth is that, even today, thirty-five years later, I still don't know what caused the uproar. I felt bad for Olaf, because I could see how embarrassed he was, and I wondered if the incident was staged for that purpose. The only thing I could say to my son was, "Go out and find her. Bring her back home. It's cold and dark outside. Where can she go?"

His immediate response was, "Oh, she'll come back!" His answer suggested this was not their first quarrel or the first time she'd run away. I'll never know for sure.

After two years of marriage, Koren and Olaf announced they were expecting their first child. What a happy time for the couple and for me as well. Beginning in November, Olaf left messages for me: "Any day now, Grandma!" Finally, he called from the hospital on November 8 with the good news. "Mom, it's a boy! Both mother and baby are doing fine."

What joy and excitement that was for me! My first (and only, as it turned out) grandchild. They named him Peter.

I prepared for the arrival of the little prince by knitting baby outfits and working on other such projects. I'd read about an old Arab custom of greeting a newborn with its weight in gold or something else of great value and presenting that to the parents. So I made a suede leather pouch and filled it with seven pounds of silver dollars, matching his birth weight. On the bag, I embroidered his name, date of birth, and his weight as a newborn. At last, the silver dollars my mother had saved for an emergency were put to good use. Had she lived long enough, I think it would have made her very proud to know her coins were entrusted to her only great grandchild.

For Peter's baptism, I flew to Wyoming and brought along his father's christening dress, which my mother had carefully wrapped in tissue paper and stored away in a box after Olaf's baptism many years before.

Mother had labeled the box, "For the Next Occasion." I had made that christening dress from my wedding gown in hopes that it would become a traditional garment that could be honored through many generations. Following Peter's christening, I asked Koren to let me keep the christening dress and save it for the next baby. Koren told me, "It belongs to Peter now, and it should stay with him." What could I do but relent?

The first tragedy that struck Olaf's marriage was Koren's sudden illness, which turned out to be cancer. At age twenty-four, this was unexpected and devastating. The process of diagnosing took many trips to doctors. Buffalo, Wyoming, was a very small town with fewer specialists than I was used to in New York City. Gradually, having exhausted the expertise of the local doctors, Olaf and Koren travelled further to larger towns with better facilities. Finally, they settled on Billings, Montana, where doctors decided Koren required open heart surgery. There, they discovered a malignant tumor that spread round her heart and which made removal impossible. The surgeons closed up her chest and prepared her for chemotherapy.

By 1981, Koren was in the midst of therapy, but she and Olaf and Peter came to New York for my second solo exhibit. I made an appointment for her at Sloan-Kettering to undergo a treatment while she visited. I was happy she was seeing one of the best oncologists here in New York and hoped for a second opinion. Koren unwillingly agreed to the appointment arranged for the day of her scheduled chemo.

The oncologists in Billings were Mayo Clinic educated and had suggested only chemo for Koren at this stage. They advised holding off on radiation for now and had recommended saving that for later, if needed. Sloan-Kettering felt she should get both treatments immediately, and it was left to Koren to choose which path to pursue.

Koren opted for the Mayo Clinic advice, and the lives of this young family were thrown into upheaval. Olaf took nearly a month off from work to stay with Koren in Billings. Peter was left with friends who offered to care for him as long as was needed. After two weeks, they turned Peter over to friends of theirs. All this was very upsetting to me. I was willing to do whatever it took and had offered to fly to Billings and stay with Koren following her surgery. Koren thought that was unnecessary.

Meanwhile, Olaf stayed with a local Lutheran pastor while Koren was in the hospital there. Then came the homecoming and all the special care she would need—at least a couple of weeks. I told Olaf I'd be willing to fly to Buffalo. He was happy to hear my willingness to help out, and agreed.

Next night, he called to say it was not a good idea for me to come and take care of Peter. "After all," he said, "twenty-seven years have gone by since you had me. Would you even know how to handle a baby?"

I was surprised and hurt. It was apparent to me that Koren did not want me to take care of little Peter. I believed then (and now) these words were not Olaf's, but hers.

So I put off my "emergency trip" and visited them at Christmas, instead. Koren was in the midst of her chemotherapy, which made her very ill. It was heartbreaking to see this young woman suffer so much. I tried my best to be helpful and do whatever I could.

During that visit, I experienced what people mean by "small town spirit." All my life, I had lived in a city where one rarely knows who lives right next door. How differently life plays itself out in a town with a population of four thousand people! It seemed everyone was involved in Koren's tragedy. From the day she came home from the hospital, people poured out their hearts in a true Christian spirit. Townsfolk arrived with cooked food. Some cooked for the family, cleaned the house, and did every conceivable errand.

This fellowship culminated on Christmas Eve. Olaf went out during the day to chop a tree, which we placed in front of the living room window and all of us decorated. As evening arrived, it began to snow. From off in the distance, far, far away, we began to hear caroling, which came closer and closer. Koren sat in her armchair in front of the window, pretty as ever. She wore a fancy negligee I'd given her and a wig her mother had sent

from Indiana. It was a solemn, heartbreaking experience. The carolers from
local churches drew nearer, and Koren's beautiful reflection appeared in
the window against the dark Christmas night sky—a night of love, of caring,
and sharing.

Koren's cancer went into remission, and life seemed to adjust to normal
again. Olaf was running the funeral home while Koren took care of the
household and brought up little Peter. Their move to Wyoming had been
a good one, or so it seemed to an outside observer. Olaf got along well with
his coworkers at Adams Funeral Home as he did with Mr. Adams himself.

Mr. Adams and his wife Norma were in their early sixties. They were
grandparents by now and had begun to plan for retirement. They had
two grown children. Their daughter and her husband were both teachers.
Their son Mark had left home some years before when he followed music
as his professional calling. He was now an accomplished concert organist,
a student of world-renowned organist Fox. Mark had settled in New Jersey
where he became music director of the well-known Newark Cathedral. From
time to time, he continued to go on concert tours. I was fortunate to have
attended two of Mark's organ concerts in New York City—one at St. Patrick's
Cathedral and another at St. Thomas Church on Fifth Avenue; and Mark
attended one of my solo shows in Westchester. Mark was a genius, and his
death from AIDS at a very young age was a great loss to the music world.

When Bill Adams hired my son, he revealed to Olaf that neither of his
children was interested in taking over the family business. He was very clear
that he was looking to hire someone who would eventually buy him out and
take over the home. Young people then were quick to flee the family coop
and choose an altogether unrelated occupation. The traditional concept of
a son taking over his father's business had begun to go by the wayside, and
Olaf felt fortunate to be an outsider who could buy into a family business.

Olaf worked conscientiously and redoubled his efforts in this business
because of the prospect of owning it one day. Over the ensuing years of his
employment there, changes occurred in the Adams family. The son-in-law
Dave, a physical education teacher, began to help out at the funeral home.
In a few years, it became very clear that he expected to be its next owner.
Olaf felt like the rug had been pulled out from under his feet.

The Adams Funeral Home was connected to Emergency Medical
Services in Buffalo. Disappointed that his dream had been dashed, Olaf
decided to take a paramedic course and become a licensed paramedic. I
continued to travel twice a year to Wyoming, usually visiting at Christmas
or Thanksgiving. I'd save both my money and my vacation days so I could
spend time with my family.

The winters were very cold in Wyoming, and the ground was always covered in deep snow. In winter, it wasn't unusual for the temperature to drop to—30°F where you could hardly breathe. You'd have to walk very fast or, better yet, run, if you didn't want to turn into an icicle! Traveling during the holidays too was challenging with crowds everywhere. Delays were the norm, and never once did my baggage arrive at the right time and place. More than once, my baggage was delivered to Wyoming on the day I returned home.

I decided the best way to avoid all this travelling angst was to visit my family in the summertime. As luck would have it, the summer of 1983 happened to be unusually hot, and the thermometer in the center of town read 103°F. As usual, I'd allotted just under a week for my visit. Koren and Olaf appeared to be fine. I'd bought Koren a pair of diamond-sapphire earrings to match my ring I'd already given her, and I baked Olaf his favorite—New York cheesecake.

The day after I arrived back home from my visit, Olaf called with shocking news. Koren had left him and had taken little Peter! How could I have been so blind to their marital strife? Why hadn't they told me to postpone my visit until later so they could work out their difficulties? But no amount of ruminating over what was done could possibly be helpful now.

So it was that in 1983, when Peter was five, Koren left my son for good. She loaded up their only car with belongings and Peter and drove to Virginia to stay with her married sister Kristie. The separation and divorce that followed was uncontested and what my son described as "amicable." It was for that reason that he agreed (against my advice) to use the same attorney as Koren to keep legal costs to a minimum.

I never asked what went wrong with their marriage, and he never elaborated. I do know five years after their divorce, Olaf had to reopen the files and sue Koren for equal visitation rights, among other matters. By then, they were angry enough with each other to be bitter enemies. So much for the "amicable" divorce.

Of course, I worried about the breakup and its effects on little Peter. I had to maintain a good relationship with Koren and stay in Peter's life at all costs. When Koren's birthday came in September and, although she and I had not communicated since she had picked up and left, I sent her a card and a check. Bingo. That was the icebreaker.

Peter was too little to understand what had taken place. In his mind, the trip with his Mommy to Virginia was just a fun trip to visit Aunt Kristie in Richmond. Of course, the return trip never materialized. His parents' separation was permanent.

Koren established herself quickly in Richmond where she planned to stay. With Kristie's help, she found a two-bedroom townhouse and a job as director of marketing in a small advertising firm. Later, I would occasionally drive to Virginia to visit with Koren and with Peter, and they came to New York for the opening of my solo shows.

When Peter was six, he began to fly to New York on his own to visit Grandma Gerda. During spring vacations and summertime, he'd board a plane in Richmond, and I'd wait for his arrival at LaGuardia. These were very happy visits for us.

Peter's visits with his dad were infrequent and complicated by the distance that separated them, the brevity of Olaf's vacation time, and the fact that he worked two jobs. The divorce agreement indicated Peter was to stay with his dad for a month each summer. But Olaf was still single at that point, and he could not care for Peter during those visits.

One summer, Peter and I visited Buffalo together, where Olaf introduced us to a registered nurse he'd met in the local hospital while on EMS duty. Her name was Pat, and she was divorced with two small children around Peter's age. I suspect her children reminded Olaf of his own son. He had spent three long lonely years since his divorce from Koren when he and Pat began to see each other. Less than a year later, they married. For Peter's part, he hung on to his father whenever they were together, more so than he did to Koren. I think he really missed his Dad.

That summer, we all went swimming in a lake near Buffalo. I noticed a dark brown mark on Olaf's chest the size of a dime. He'd had a very small birthmark there when he was born. But the mark I noticed that day looked much larger than what I recalled. I told him he ought to see his doctor, but it didn't strike him as urgent. I completely forgot about it myself once I returned home.

Six months later, I was watching the election of President Nixon, when Olaf called to tell me the mark had gotten much larger and had started to bleed. Finally, he had gone to the doctor who told him it looked like melanoma. I felt like lightning had struck. I knew the news was not good. It was bad—very bad news.

Almost immediately after this conversation with Olaf, the phone rang again. It was Koren calling at the worst possible moment. Clearly, she detected the angst in my voice and kept asking me what was wrong and whether there was something wrong with Olaf.

"Yes," I said, "it's Olaf. But you must promise me not to mention it to anyone if I tell you."

Koren promised, and I trusted her.

"Olaf has cancer," I told Koren. "He made me promise to keep it to myself until he is over the shock and prepared to speak about it himself."

I was planning to visit Olaf and his family for Christmas the following month and bring eleven-year-old Peter with me. Shortly before our trip,

Koren announced, "My son has the right to know what's going on with his father and should be prepared to face it when they meet."

I begged Koren not to do this, given Peter was still very young. In fact, Olaf had requested that he himself be allowed to carry out what he saw as his own responsibility to disclose such tragic news to his son and in his own time. Koren knew this.

I should have known better than to break the trust Olaf had placed in me by telling Koren, to begin with. For her part, Koren should also have honored her promise to me. I felt very betrayed, and I have yet to get over both the guilt I feel for disclosing Olaf's condition to Koren and my disappointment in her for sharing this information with Peter.

I peddled carefully between Koren and Olaf, trying to stay on good terms with them both. In the long run, I learned one cannot befriend individuals from opposing enemy camps. I justified my position to Olaf insisting that I'd do anything to keep a positive relationship with my grandson. I hoped he would understand, and for a while he seemed to accept that.

In 1989, I took Peter and went to visit Olaf, Pat, and his new family in Colorado where they'd recently moved from Wyoming. Olaf had been operated on and was now on chemotherapy. The doctors found his melanoma had advanced to stage IV. He was very sick, but still working.

The atmosphere was thick in their home, and Pat hardly talked to me. I sensed she was trying to avoid me whenever possible. I couldn't figure out whether to attribute this to something going on in their marriage, to our visit, or if it was just Olaf's illness. But it was Christmastime, and I pretended not to notice the depressed mood that pervaded the household. Olaf was working extra shifts so he could take time off between holidays, and he was hardly ever at home. There was no holiday spirit or preparation going on in the home.

"How about a Christmas tree?" I asked Pat.

"There's one outside lying in the snow," she said. "Olaf brought it home and left it there. I'm not touching it."

I decided to intervene. "Pat, I've come a long way to spend Christmas with my son and his family. You can't spoil Christmas for the kids and for me."

I asked a neighborhood teen to help bring in the tree and set it up. Now, we could decorate! Then, on Christmas Eve, we all went to church.

Christmas morning was filled with excitement. The children had fun, and we all had many gifts under the tree. Most, I had brought from New York. The gifts for Olaf and Pat seemed not to please them for reasons I couldn't determine.

The telephone rang as we were opening gifts. It was Koren asking for Peter. After she spoke with him, she asked to talk to me. Suddenly, Olaf became someone I did not recognize as my own son. I had never known him to yell at me or to raise his voice at me in anger. But now, he was irate about my support for Koren and our friendship. Before I could speak, Pat chimed in as well. I couldn't imagine what I might say.

Later, when Olaf and I were alone, I reminded him of my motives for keeping a relationship with Peter's mother. After all, Koren had the power to distance me from my grandson, and I had good reason to believe she would have done exactly that. Especially so, considering the post-divorce issues she had with Olaf.

It was a very difficult Christmas—as it happened, the last I would spend with Olaf. Two years later, he died. That was more than twenty years ago, and even today I'm consumed with guilt. Was I more concerned about losing my grandson than about hurting my son? Was it unfair of me to maintain a relationship with Peter's mother at all costs? Was I careless in failing to remind Olaf again and again to go see a doctor? Would earlier intervention have saved his life?

Only God knows the answers to all of my questions.

When Koren had left my son for the last time, she overlooked the treasured box that contained the christening gown and left it behind with Olaf. In 1991 when Olaf died, his second wife Pat refused to return the outfit to Peter, to Koren, or even to me. Though I'm certain the dress has no meaning for Pat, its disappearance from my family represents a great loss.

IX

My Last Trip to Latvia/Travels with Koren

In 2008, I looked forward with great excitement to the grand opening of the Diaspora Art Returns. I didn't want to miss this once-in-a-lifetime event! I could attend the opening and visit my homeland once more. It was a dream come true. But with my physical strength in decline, as it was, I didn't dare travel alone.

On a visit to Florida where Koren and her husband Greg Rhoads lived, we talked about the Diaspora Exhibit. "Why don't you ask Koren to travel with you?" Greg asked me. What a great idea! So I asked, and she immediately began to consult with her doctors to see how risky such a trip might be.

The first time Koren's cancer went into remission, she had more than ten years before it recurred in the midnineties. Although it took a different form when it returned, she again underwent chemo, and, this time, radiation treatment, as well. By now, her second bout with cancer was also in remission although she had occasional health problems that would crop up, requiring her to remain under strict medical supervision.

Apparently, her doctors relented to her trip, and she began planning while I made preparations. We would begin in Riga with a ten-day stay at the Hotel de Rome. From there, we would travel by car the two-hour trip to Valmiera. We would attend the opening and stay in a small hotel another day or two, then return to the airport in Riga to fly home. Anticipating the many things we would do and places we'd visit was very exciting, but I had to be sure Koren and I were comfortable. By now, I was often using a cane, especially for longer walks. So I bought a second one for myself, just in case I misplaced mine or left it somewhere.

Finally, the day came. Koren arrived from Florida for our overseas flight. We boarded the plane and had just settled into our seats when Koren confessed that her condition was borderline and her doctors had agreed to her trip with reluctance. There was no time now to worry about that. As she finished confiding this point, we were already in the air and on our way.

In Riga, we were met at the airport and greeted with flowers by my first cousin Astrīda and her son Dr. Igor Chashin. This was the first time I'd met Astrīda's son. Then Koren and I settled into our hotel suite and took a very long nap!

The Hotel de Rome, now designated a five-star hotel, had always been the most elegant and most expensive hotel in Riga. That was true even prior to World War II when foreign diplomats and other dignitaries stayed there. It had been destroyed by fire during the war and was now rebuilt on the same site located on the main boulevard—Aspāzijas Boulevard—across from the National Opera House. It had the same front portal as the original. The interior had been modernized, but it was just as elegant as it ever had been. Our room overlooked the most famous "Brīvības Piemineklis" (the Freedom Monument) erected in 1934. We could also see the wide Boulevards with their greenery and flowers, as well as the Opera, which we called Our White House.

Of course, directly across the street was a McDonald's with its tacky bright lights. There were tables and chairs placed outside, and we could see that McDonald's was a favored hangout for the young people. It was open twenty-four hours a day. Customers played music and performed break dancing until well into the early morning hours. It was early August, and the weather was beautiful. It was sunny in the daytime and a little cooler at night. Koren and I would open the windows and close the heavy brocade drapes at night just to keep out the noise.

We had breakfast in the hotel dining room, served smorgasbord style with a sinful selection of virtually everything you could imagine. Even we diet-conscious girls couldn't avoid taking advantage of all the excess. By the third morning (and being the older and wiser of the two), I said to Koren, "We better stop making pigs of ourselves lest we outgrow our jeans before we get home." It was a halfhearted warning at best, and I don't think either of us took it seriously. Koren even snuck out once for a malted I'm pretty sure she got at McDonald's.

On my earlier trips to Latvia, I had stayed with my dear cousin Edgars Zīle who occupied my grandparents' former apartment in Midtown. In honor of our first such reunion (after fifty-eight years), Edgars renamed Grandma's living room "Gerda's Room." Edgars and his wife Valija fussed and fawned over me at every opportunity.

Edgars and I had been very close as children. He was five years my junior, which made a big difference when we were children. He and his brother Zigismunds (three years older than Edgars) had been like brothers to me. I was always taller and the leader, and I often thought of Edgars as a "nuisance" because he used to hang on to me all the time. But what an impression I'd left upon him! Now, he remembered every detail from our past—my parents, where we lived, our summers spent together, and all the things we had done together.

During the Soviet occupation, most larger apartments that had been occupied before the war by single families were converted to multifamily dwellings that accommodated "one family per room." That was the law. I remember having seen this when I visited one of my former classmates in her family's seven-room apartment. The front door had six name plates, with a door bell for each. My own family had been very fortunate to be able to keep Grandma's five-room apartment for themselves because they had fulfilled the quota requirements with four persons registered there. There had been Tante Ella and her two sons, Zigismunds and Edgars, as well as Grandma Elizabeth who was still alive at the time. What a treat it had been to visit with Edgars and relive old memories from childhood.

During my first visit in 1992, Edgars drove me to visit the home my family and I had once lived in. He and I had to use a street map to locate the house because so much had changed beyond recognition. The two-story family house was still there where we used to rent the upper floor and where the owners—friends of ours—lived downstairs. For us, it had been a brand-new house, and my mother had participated in how the apartment should look.

The main entrance door now had seven or eight doorbells and nameplates written in Latvian and Russian. I hesitated, and Edgars said, "Listen, since we're already here, why don't we ring one of the upstairs bells where you used to live?" and he pointed to one that had a Latvian name.

So I did. An elderly Latvian couple came to the door. I introduced myself and told them the reason for our visit. Immediately, they invited us in. Upon entering the hallway, my impression was one of neglect. There were holes in the tile floors, and the doors had no handles. The many layers of chipping paint on the doors, and walls revealed all the previous colors. The doors leading into separate rooms were all closed. As the couple led us to the kitchen, each door would open one at a time just enough for someone to peer out and see who was there.

My room, a good-sized corner room with two wide windows, was split in half by a dividing wall, and two apartments had been made out of my room where two families now lived. Same thing with what used to be our dining room.

I asked how long the couple had lived there. "We came in October 1944." That was just two months after Mami and I left.

While I talked with the couple, Edgars looked around to see if he could spot a piece of our furniture. But it had been almost sixty years after all. There wasn't a chance of that. Everything was different now.

Back at his place, Edgars would not dream of letting me stay in a hotel. That would be an insult to his generous hospitality. I contacted several old classmates and was going to invite "the girls" to lunch at a nice restaurant.

When Edgars heard of my plans, he became very sad and said, "I don't understand you, Gerdiņa. Why don't you want to invite your guests to our home instead of taking them to some restaurant?"

It had not occurred to me that Edgars would be offended. I certainly did not expect him and Valija to entertain my friends as well as myself. The economy was in shambles, and the stores were empty. Times were very difficult for them, and there was no recovery in sight. The simplest of goods, but especially luxury items, required Soviet style transactions where you simply had to know somebody in order to get what you wanted. I had no idea how Edgars managed to get all the goodies for my party although he admitted to having waited in line three hours to buy the champagne!

I tried hard to be as generous as I could, and I began to supplement their income to ensure that they could afford the medical supplies and other things they needed. I wanted to help them and managed to do so although even my resources were stretched pretty thin until my own circumstances changed in 2004 following the death of my friend Josephine. But I was always guided by the thought that "If there's a will, there must be a way." Edgars and Valija had lost so much and struggled so hard, I was grateful the Lord made it possible for me to be able to help. By 1995, when I returned to Latvia for my second time, the economy had begun to perk up, and American dollars would buy much more.

When Koren and I arrived in 2008, things had changed dramatically. Edgars had passed away, his lungs having been damaged from the many years he worked in the Siberian coal mines. Valija was no longer in good health, and her grandson Gatis Čapass had moved in along with his girlfriend Samantha in order to make life easier for Valija and to help her pay her monthly maintenance and utilities. Of course "Gerda's Room" was no longer available.

While Edgars was alive, he and Valija had somehow managed with the higher pension Edgars received, having worked in Siberia from the age of sixteen, following his deportation. Even so, the purchase of medications not covered by their government plan had to come out of pocket. But now, without Edgars' pension, Valija received very little.

I had chosen to stay at the Hotel de Rome because of its great location right in the center of town where most everything we wanted to see was in walking distance. We had access to the Old Town of Riga—Vecrīga—which had recently celebrated its eight hundredth birthday and was now a tourist attraction. I wanted to show Koren as much as I could of the town where I was born and grew up. Koren had to make frequent stops to rest, and I was not able to walk much myself. But we complemented each other and had a very good time making fun of ourselves.

By now, I had known Koren thirty-two years, and we both had mixed memories to reflect on. She and I had visited often, but only as guests in each other's homes. I had wondered if traveling together for two weeks could actually work. We are both strong, independent women, and such traits can easily lead to conflict. As it turned out, my concerns were completely unfounded. She and I got along very well.

I had two lists of things to do while in Latvia—one list of "must dos" and another labeled "time permitting." My main goal, of course, was to attend the opening of our Diaspora Exhibit and take an active role in the realization of our dream for a historical museum in Latvia, which would show works Latvian artists created outside of Latvia since 1944.

Another "must do" was to visit two of our cemeteries, which is an old and deep-seated tradition to honor our ancestors by visiting their graves. One of these was the Matthews Cemetery (Matīsa kapi) in Riga, where my mother's family is buried. My father and relatives on his side of my family are buried in the Russian Orthodox Cemetery in Dubulti, a sea resort outside of Riga. Both cemeteries are hundreds of years old, still exceptionally well kept, with trees, blooming bushes, live flowers, and greenery everywhere.

In Latvia, the grave is built up from ground level about six to eight inches. Upkeep is usually done by the families. About once a week, someone waters the plot, removes the dead leaves and other debris and, before leaving, rakes the sandy walkways around the grave and leaves it with a design. Koren was very taken by the parklike setting and the many visitors, unlike what we usually see here in the States.

Memorial Day in Latvia (Mirušo Pieminu Diena) in the Month of November—a Flashback

I'm maybe nine or ten years old and walking with my parents in the cemetery. It's late in the afternoon and very cold. A light snow starts falling and begins to cover the ground with a fluffy white blanket. Today is a very special day. It's our Annual Memorial Day, the day we remember and celebrate the lives of those who are no longer with us. It's not quite dark yet as we enter the cemetery through the big black iron gates and notice some flickering lights from candles placed on the graves. By the time we reach our family plot, more and more lights become visible. The graves that we pass—it seems like all of them—are decorated with green long-needle pine branches. Dressed for the occasion!

We place our white candles on the graves while my father tries to light them with his cigarette lighter. It seems so quiet all around us. Nothing is moving, yet a light breeze once in a while touches the ground and makes some of the lighted candles flicker. Will the flames die? No, not on this special night! In a second or two, the flickering stops, and the flames straighten up and return to their original glorious glow.

I look around, and all I see is an ocean of lights. The air is filled with a scent—a mixture of burning candles and fresh pine needles. Before leaving, we gather around a grave, holding hands. The burning candles reflect light and shadows on our faces. Peace on earth.

On our way home, we stop at my grandparents' home for a glass of tea and a snack. Then we catch a streetcar right on the corner of the block where my grandma lives, which takes us back to our home in the suburbs.

On Sunday morning, Koren and I attended Sunday Service in the St. Peter's Evangelic Lutheran Church where my family has worshiped for three generations. I was confirmed there in 1940 during the first Soviet invasion of Latvia. This gothic church was built in the thirteenth century, and its wood steeple was claimed to be the highest in Europe at the time. According to historians, St. Peter's was destroyed by fire several times during the past eight centuries and, each time, rebuilt once again. The last fire in 1941 burned it to the ground when the German Army crossed our borders and advanced into Russia at the beginning of World War II.

At one time, St. Peter's was the pride of Riga for its pure gothic style and beautiful interior. The walls had been decorated with old large white-and-gold family crests and plaques honoring dignitaries of the City of Riga—both clergy and city patriarchs. All that was destroyed in the last fire. From where my family lived across the River Daugava, I watched for three days as the church burned. On the fourth day, the smoldering steeple slowly disappeared into the church interior.

During the Soviet occupation, some rebuilding took place up to the second floor. The purpose of the rebuilding was to turn the church into a concert hall. I had seen the rebuilt church in 1992 on my first visit back. The steeple had been replaced with its famous golden weathercock at the top. The interior walls were of plain red bricks that had an unfinished look, and the inside of the structure seemed bare.

One of our famous writers and poets, Kārlis Skalbe, wrote this poem:

Draugs, kur laimīgs esi bijis, neatgriezies vairs—
Tā kā saulē lietus lijis . . .
Vakar bij' un šodien nav.

Laiks ir visu pārmainījis,
Šodien viss ir citāds jau.

Loosely translated from Latvian:

My friend, don't go back where you were happy once,
It will be like raindrops falling in the sunshine;
What you had yesterday is gone today,
Time has changed everything,
And all is different now.

Koren and I were invited to dinner by my first cousin Dr. Sibilla Pālena and her retired husband Juris. That visit turned out more like a family gathering. There was cousin Astrīda with her son Igor and his wife Dr. Irisa. My other first cousin Edgars Brutāns was there—a retired civil engineer. Sibilla's daughter was there with her three boys.

The younger generation all spoke English—Igor, Irisa, Ginta, as did Sibilla. I had to interpret for the rest. It was such a pleasant afternoon visit. They all liked Koren, and she was impressed with my father's family.

Another invitation came from Edgars's widow, Valija. Her daughter Inese Čapass was a CPA for L'Oreal in Riga, and she was there with her two sons Mārtiņš and Gatis with his girlfriend Samantha. Valija looked tired and very lonesome. Still, she and her family provided plenty of hospitality for which Latvia is quite well-known. The following year, Inese wrote me that her mother had passed away in her sleep. Valija was a very kind woman.

While we were in Riga, Koren and I also did a good bit of sightseeing but not as much as I would have liked. We visited the National Crafts Museum, one of my favorites, with textiles, tapestries, wood, and porcelain. Another place on our must-see list was the Occupation Museum, 1940-2000." Here, explicitly captioned pictures, which sometimes took up entire walls, told the story of the sixty-year occupation of Latvia. There were many donated objects that had survived deportation to Siberia and which had somehow found their way home. Entire installations were comprised of replicas of slave labor barracks, self-made utensils, and hand-carved wooden plates and cups. There were also letters written on birch tree bark.

Of course, I had visited that museum several times before and was more emotionally prepared to see it again and live through the ugly past one step at a time. Koren, on the other hand, had only heard of the occupation from stories I told her through the years. What she saw in the museum was overwhelming for her.

We visited the Alexander Nevsky Russian Orthodox Church in Midtown too. This is where my grandfather Alexander Semēnowitch was baptized in 1865. This church is very small, but one of the most beautiful Orthodox churches in Riga. Somehow, it had survived the Communist plunder; and its gold icons, crosses decorated with precious stones, and old religious paintings had been miraculously spared.

In stark contrast was the grand Russian Orthodox Cathedral in Riga, which had been robbed blind. All that had been left were bare walls. The crosses had been sawed off the steeples, and the cathedral was turned into a restaurant, not unlike many other houses of worship that became movie theaters, coffee houses, or libraries.

The National Opera House is closed in the summer months, but concerts are given in halls outside the city in various province towns. Sibilla had bought tickets for a concert in Dzintari, a sea resort outside of Riga. On the program were favorite opera arias performed by three international vocalists. The Summer Concert Hall is built in the shape of a mushroom with a flat roof and open sides. The concert took place on a very warm afternoon, but the cool sea breeze blew in from the ocean. The opera music was beautiful. I closed my eyes and stepped back in time. I was young again.

On our way to the concert in Dzintari, Koren and
I took a stroll along the seashore

Koren and I also attended a concert at the Dome Cathedral and another at St. Peter's Church. Of course, we did some shopping from street vendors along the Boulevards—mostly souvenirs and little gifts to bring home. Koren had a fabulous time moving from one vendor stand to the next. There were Latvian silversmiths who still made reproductions of ancient jewelry pieces using sterling silver and amber, which is one of Latvia's semiprecious stones.

Amber is a brownish-yellow, translucent fossil resin that hardens in the ground under the ocean floor over hundreds or even thousands of years. In Latvia, amber was first discovered through archaeological digs along the shores of the Baltic Sea. But it can still be found in the sand along the seashore, especially after a storm.

Finally, it was time for the primary aim of my trip—the opening of our "Diaspora Art Returns" at the Valmiera Museum. Sibilla and her daughter Ginta with her own five-month-old nursing baby Krišjānis drove us to Valmiera where we had reservations to stay for two nights. There, we discovered that Valmiera was about to celebrate its 750th birthday that weekend. Had I known that in advance, we might have stayed in Valmiera a couple more days. Not only was this a grand celebration, the town of Valmiera is very pretty.

At the museum, works for the exhibit had been shipped to Riga from all over the globe and arrived on time in Valmiera, ready to hang in the museum. Dr. Kalmīte made sure we had a beautiful catalogue, printed in Latvia in cooperation with the museum. That alone was an enormous accomplishment!

The museum itself is just two stories high, but it appeared much larger as the consequence of how our show was hung. Most paintings and sculptures were on the ground floor. Works under glass were on the second floor. My painting, *Exit*, hung on the wall opposite the first floor main entrance—an exceptional placement for its subdued palette and the shadowy figure reflecting my departed son Olaf.

My cousin Sibilla greeted me at the opening with a beautiful bouquet of roses. The opening was well attended and included the Mayor of Valmiera and other art-world dignitaries. There were local and overseas art historians—among them, Eleonora Šturma from New York and Māra Lāce, director of the Latvian National Art Museum in Riga. Twenty of the participating artists actually arrived from various countries—USA, England, Canada, and Australia.

The museum provided a very nice reception with bountiful food and drink. The exhibit was unique. For the first time ever, the diverse body of works represented only exile artists. The title of the show was "Tēvu Zemei—Latvijai" (Dedicated to Our Homeland—Latvia).

When Sibilla's daughter Ginta arrived by car to take us back to Riga Airport, I was surprised to find the whole family there. Sibilla, Ginta and her baby Krišjānis, Astrīda and her son Igor with his wife Irisa had all shown up to wish us Bon Voyage. Once again, as is customary in Latvia, they all brought us farewell gifts. At the airport, we had time for a cup of coffee and small talk. Then Koren and I boarded the Polish Airline Lot, and I said good-bye to my homeland, most likely for the last time.

On the day of our departure from the International Airport in Riga, the whole family came to wish us Bon Voyage!
First row (left to right): Myself, cousins Sibilla and Astrida.
Second row: Koren, Astrida's son Igor and Sibilla's daughter Ginta.

Following this two month exhibition in Valmiera, the show traveled for two years to eighteen different venues in Latvia, including St. Peter's Church in Riga.

Thus was laid the foundation for a permanent art center in Latvia with reasonable expectations that Valmiera might become the permanent seat for the Diaspora Museum we envisioned. Sadly, this plan has since fallen victim to the global economic crisis, which has had a devastating effect on Latvia.

The original collection is now temporarily stored in a museum in Cēsis, an hour and a half drive North of Riga. Cēsis is a smaller town than Valmiera but perhaps better known for its artistic endeavors and activities in support of the arts. They have an annual art festival, the only one of its kind in Latvia. In 2006 when that festival celebrated the eight hundredth birthday of Cēsis, mention was made of this celebratory event in the UNESCO annual calendar.

The GSLA has since been invited by the town of Cēsis to consider them for a permanent Diaspora Art Returns Museum. Negotiations between GSLA and the Cēsis Town Council are still ongoing.

As for me, in addition to Exit, five additional large acrylic paintings of mine have been added to the collection of the future Diaspora Art Museum. Four of my monotypes have been accepted into the permanent collection of the Latvian National Art Museum Arsenals in Riga.

X

My Grandson Peter

Letter to Peter

A couple of weeks after your father's death, I received a phone call from a life insurance company asking me the whereabouts of Peter Dobrzanski. I asked what the call was about, and the caller said they could not release information to me except to say that my name appeared on one of their policies. I asked if they would respond with a yes or no to a simple question. The caller agreed, and I asked, "Is this about a death benefit?" "Yes," was the answer I was hoping to hear. Hallelujah!

I gave them the Richmond address I had for Koren and called her immediately. You were twelve years old at that time, and Koren was preparing for her second marriage.

When your father was in the last year of his life, his illness was progressing rapidly, and he had little hope left. We kept in close contact by telephone, and I had some man-to-man talks with him about whether his important papers were in order "just in case." He assured me they were more or less.

I knew his relationship with your mother was at its lowest point, and I asked if he had taken care of you in his testament. His answer was vague, and his tone was defensive. I couldn't be sure what he meant or what he had actually done. I worried that you might be left out of his will—a needless rejection. I prayed to God that wouldn't happen.

I knew from the call I had gotten that there was an insurance policy. What I learned from Koren, which was not much, was that your father had two policies—one in your name for $50,000 and another policy for his wife Pat.

Once Olaf was gone, Pat tried to replace your name with her own as sole beneficiary of the $50,000 policy. She claimed Olaf intended to make that change but never got around to doing so. But the judge ruled that "the beneficiary's name on a life insurance policy is carved in stone except for very rare cases." What a relief!

Many things happened that you may not remember or may never have known about during your childhood. After seven years of marriage, your mother left your father. And while I never questioned the reasons, she must have been very unhappy. I do know your father was very distraught when your mother took you and left. He always worried about you and your whereabouts and who was taking care of you when your mother was at work. Remember, you were only five years old! He lived with nightmares for a very long time.

He loved you very much and missed you. And although he visited with you in Richmond a couple of times—and maybe that wasn't enough—he tried to arrange to have you stay with him during the summer. But before he married Pat, he could not care for you properly at your young age of seven or eight while maintaining the long working hours his job required.

I know he believed that marrying Pat would solve this problem. He looked forward to having a family again and having you as part of that family. He was wrong to believe that Pat would be a caring and loving mother, both to her own children and to you. Pat was not a nice person. But he did love you and felt responsible for you and your future.

He purchased the $50,000 life insurance policy in your name and paid monthly premiums for years in spite of the difficulties he faced. And he never mentioned this to anyone, not even to me on his deathbed. That was my son.

You meant a lot to him. That, I know.

From a Child to a Man

As a child, Peter visited me every summer, and we always had a great time. Of course, that was before he became a teenager, and I knew he'd have better things to do with his time than to visit Grannie in New York.

He joined the ROTC. while in high school and graduated in 1997. Upon the recommendation of his ROTC captain, he was admitted to Virginia Tech, one of the finest colleges in the country—and with a four-year scholarship, no less. What a proud day for me to celebrate his success. There is an old Latvian proverb: "Cilvēks domā, Dievs dara." Translated, this means "Man thinks, God acts."

After the first semester, Peter began to fall behind in his studies. Ultimately, he did not graduate from VT. The bar for success was too high for him. His mother and stepfather Greg drove to Virginia to try to persuade him to persevere. After all, the first year in college is always a time of adjustment. It is difficult for most students, especially those who are away from home for the first time—away from family, friends, girlfriends. But Peter could not be persuaded. Instead, he dropped out of college and returned home.

Little Peter (10 months old) safe in his father's arms in Buffalo, Wyoming where he was born in 1978.

As far back as I can remember, Peter loved the military. Here, at age 4 in 1982, he began training for the real thing!

Life had changed for Peter. The first reunion with his dad after having left Buffalo was Christmas 1983 when Olaf visited him in Virginia.

In 1989 I travelled with Peter to Colorado to spend Christmas with his Dad. In pursuit of his dream of serving in the U.S. Army he would wear only Army fatigues.

In high school, Peter joined the Navy ROTC

I took this very hard. To give up such a prized opportunity did not make sense to me, believing as I did that fortitude and perseverance could overcome any adversity. But we are who we are, and we all have options and make choices that dictate consequences we then have to live with. I even wondered if his father's life insurance money had given him a false sense of secure independence.

At home in Florida, the "house rules"—the imposed curfew, especially—became much too strict for Peter to live with, and he ultimately moved out of his family's home. He bought a house and rented out half to a roommate to help pay the mortgage. He also got a clerical job in a home security company and enrolled in a local college to study for an associate degree.

Though I travelled to Jacksonville several times to visit Koren, and often saw Peter, the details of his life were never really discussed. Peter was always polite and charming, but over the years, I began to miss the warm and personal touches. Telephone contact and greeting cards seemed to become less and less frequent. Little flames tend to die out if they're not nurtured and tended to after all.

I confess to holding two-way conversations with myself in order to get to the bottom of things that perplex me. I call these sessions "conversations with the most intelligent person around." Since I live alone, this allows me the luxury of airing my opinions, if not frankly solving a problem. I certainly don't want to lose my grandson. He's all that I have. The thought alone hurts too much. But as time passes and nothing changes, I begin to lose hope. After all, Peter is no longer a little boy. He's a grown man now and lives life as he sees fit.

But one day in the spring of 2006, he called me! "Guess what, Grandma."

My first thought was that he was getting married. I knew he'd been dating several girls, but there had not been a serious relationship that I knew about. Even he used to say, "Hey, I just met my next ex-girlfriend."

"I just signed up with the U.S. Army for five years," he announced. "I want to become an army ranger."

Well, that certainly took me by surprise! Not a word to anyone before this. Not even his parents. And here it was signed, sealed, and delivered.

For years, even when Peter was little, he used to love wearing military fatigues. When he'd visit me, I'd take him to the local Army & Navy Store where he would spend hours looking through old Army stuff. And naturally, Grandma was delighted to buy something for him to take home.

On one occasion when he was eleven, he had his heart set on an Army knife. I thought he was old enough to handle a knife responsibly. Of course, the knife I had in mind was more like a Swiss Army knife, perhaps. But Peter had in mind a nice-looking knife with at least a six-inch blade! It was a little pricier than I had in mind anyway, so I told him it was more than I'd planned to spend.

"Don't worry, Grandma," he said. "When I grow up and you will be old, if you're still alive, I'll buy stuff for you." I wonder if he remembers that.

When the day came for Peter to fly home, I drove him to LaGuardia Airport. We found ourselves in a traffic jam on the Whitestone Bridge and arrived very late. As we rushed through the security gate, an agent spotted the knife in Peter's backpack and detained us because of the "assault weapon" Peter was carrying. I had to fill out several forms that explained why Peter was carrying this knife. The agent put it into a safely sealed envelope and told Peter to retrieve it in Jacksonville.

So the signs of his interest had been there for years. But now, I had mixed feelings about Peter's decision to join the army. I'm certainly all for the military because of my family history. My husband, my father, and my grandfather as well were all military men after all. But my reservations for Peter were based upon timing. It was 2006, and we were embroiled in a difficult war in the Middle East as the consequence of 9/11.

On the day Peter graduated from Ranger School, he was visited by his family. Here, he is surrounded by his adoring siblings—Olivia, Adam, and Camille.

On this special day, Peter is getting pinned with the Ranger insignia by his stepfather Greg Rhoads.

But Peter was now twenty-eight years old and was undoubtedly seeking to find success and security. He had not finished his education, and his job with the Home Security Company was less than an optimal career opportunity. Even in matters of the heart, Peter had yet to find a long-term relationship.

I invited him to New York to visit before shipping out. He made it a long weekend, and I will always be grateful to him for coming to see me before he went off to war. He looked well and was in good spirits. It seemed to me he was very patriotic in his responsibility to fight for freedom of country and to prevent another 9/11. I was proud of him.

After his visit, I felt assured that he'd made the right choice. He knew what he wanted to do and was going to do it. I imagined the military discipline could flatten out some of the wrinkles from his past, assuming he reached his goal of becoming an army ranger. Still, I worried about whether he knew what he was getting himself into by setting for himself such a high standard. I certainly didn't. I'm sure becoming a Ranger takes both physical and intellectual strength, as well as a strong will and capacity to endure any environment or circumstance. Not to mention a burning desire to reach one's goal.

Here, Peter is returning from one of his nightly patrols in Afghanistan. He has reached his goal to serve our beloved country. God Bless America!

For the next five years, I followed Peter's whereabouts through e-mails sent to his mother, which she forwarded to me. He was deployed five times to war zones—three times to Iraq and twice to Afghanistan. He has been awarded the Purple Heart. On December 4, 2011, he was discharged from the army at his choice, having fulfilled his five-year commitment.

Between deployments, he finally met the girl of his dreams. Her name is Lindsey Catarino. After a short whirlwind courtship, they became engaged and were married in Maui, Hawaii, on December 10, 2011.

In one of Peter's e-mails to the family written just before his discharge, he wrote, "Pretty soon I'll be home and starting the process of getting out of the army on the fourth of December! It's hard to believe that it's been five years since I went off to basic training. So much has transpired in that time, and I'm truly glad that I got the chance to have all the experiences that I lived through—good *and* bad! I know that for the rest of my life, I will walk around with my head held high. And most importantly, I'll never have to wonder what it was like or if I had what it takes."

Bravo, Peter!

Epilogue

One morning, I looked in the mirror and saw the face of a middle-aged woman. I asked myself, "All these long years—where have they gone?" I realized then, as I do now, that I'm inclined to dwell on life's big disappointments more than to enjoy my true achievements, the greatest of which, as I think of it now, was to earn my college degree at Columbia. In today's world, such a degree may be nothing special. But then, only 7 percent of women had actually earned one!

I had already accomplished a lot but never had my work been fulfilling as I had dreamed that it would be. I regretted having not finished my master's degree and still imagined my true "place" somewhere in the field of medicine. Even today, when I enter a hospital or meet with a doctor, I feel like that's where I ought to be. As a young woman, I always *knew* beyond hope there would be a chance to have a career in medicine. But it's been hard to confront a sense of finality on what was to be an unattainable dream.

This was not the life I planned to live. Many wishes and dreams—my mother's and my own—did not become a reality. Sometimes I wonder where the journey went wrong. Was it the nearly three-year delay in admission to University of Munich that ultimately made medicine an impossible career choice? Was it the twists and turns of seeking, finding, and waiting for the right opportunity to emigrate? Had the promise of a future life with Klemens and his support of my own aspirations been just my own hopeful delusion?

When I looked in that mirror, I had not yet realized the key to my happiness was handed to me the day I climbed those five flights to Ted Davis's Studio on Seventeenth Street in New York. Over time, it was art that replaced all I had lost and gave meaning where that seemed to be missing.

When my son Olaf was struck by cancer, and hope for recovery became an illusion, the only place my aching heart could find refuge was in my studio where I hid from reality. But when I would go into my kitchen to make a cup of coffee, reality always returned.

It seems to me now that the time has come to look back on my life and consider what I've achieved and what I am leaving behind when departure day comes. Instead, what immediately comes to mind are the important people who've influenced my life and the mementos that remind me of them.

My mother, of course, was my constant companion and surely the single most important person to shape my own aspirations and goals. As an only child, when I would beg Mami to let me join the Girl Scouts where I could make friends like the other girls did, she would always remind me: "You don't have the time, Gerdiņa, for outside activities. You must concentrate on your academic work, your music, and foreign languages." She was right, of course. There were never enough hours in the day to accomplish all I imagined.

I had just entered Gymnasium when Mami had her first nervous breakdown. As I think of it now, it seems to me the entwining of the rest of her life with my own likely began with that illness. I would read to her after school to keep her alert and interested in the world around her. One of our favorites was the Latvian translation of Margaret Mitchell's *Gone with the Wind*—a two-volume book I pulled from our shelves, which was bound in Kelly green linen.

In our home, we purchased books rather than borrowing them from the library, because my father was concerned—as were others at the time—about picking up contagious diseases from books that were handled by the general public. When Mami and I fled our country, I remember holding these two beautiful volumes, trying to decide whether to take them with me or not. Instead, I packed "Latvju Lirika," the poetry book given to me in 1940 by my dear cousin Zigi on my confirmation day.

This book of poems miraculously survived its own travels—first in my backpack on the refugee boat from Riga Harbor to Danzig. Later, in Austria, it survived its ten-year burial in a wooden box during the soviet occupation, after which it was rescued and made its way across the Atlantic to the New World where my mother and I had begun our new life. Today, it rests on my bookshelf here in Mount Vernon, New York. That very special book of poetry and I are both survivors, and its poems serve as a constant reminder to me of the past that I've lived myself.

From the day we fled Riga, Mother and I walked hand in hand to make sure we were not separated by falling bombs in cities that burned. There were many families who did lose children as family members became separated from one another, especially during air raids. So Mami and I held hands as we marched in an endless stream of thousands of refugees.

By nature, I am not a fighter and never an aggressor—far more a dreamer than a realist. When the war turned our lives upside down, I took on responsibilities for which I had no experience. I had grown up sheltered and protected by my mother from all that was evil. Suddenly—virtually overnight—I had to confront reality. And so that's what I did.

Most of whatever I have accomplished in life has been of necessity and for sheer survival. Today, I am a painter with an ever-present burning desire to create. I began that life, as most newcomers do, full of excitement, expectations and hope for successful results. I have learned not to despair when success eludes me but to hold tight to the knowledge that I've given it my very best.

For one of my last solo shows, I was interviewed by Katherine Ann Samon, editor of the local *Larchmont Gazette*. This is what she wrote:

> Sky is the limit for ambitious artist GERDA ROZE at 85! At age 40, Ms. Roze began her art classes and found her voice . . . . The depth and movement of her canvasses seem as much an exploration of the universe as they do a poetic life she has kept under wraps.

It is true that my fulfillment came late in life but not surprising to me. Other important milestones have always seemed to me to come late. I call it "catching the last car of the last train."

Circumstances and events in my life brought on by the war have left indelible, deep lines in my face and have burdened my soul forever. Surviving a tragedy or traumatic experience leaves a wound that, at best, heals with a scar. With sufficient time, it may no longer feel sharply painful. Healing can sometimes occur to the point where the wound itself disappears into the past, and maybe no one else even knows that it's there. But the scar still serves as a constant reminder of personal emotional trauma. Even now, I have nightmares in which I fear being followed, caught, and tortured by the Soviet Secret Police. On those nights, I awaken in a sweat and cannot fall back to sleep, for fear the dream will continue.

In many ways—maybe in most—my journey has been a bumpy ride from beginning to end. I think of that train trip in 1929—the one I took with my mother from Riga to Olaine where she and I found ourselves alone on the platform as the train pulled out of the station. Guided by her determination and fortitude, we made our arduous trek through the countryside to reach our ultimate destination.

Because that's what I remember right now, I suppose that accounts in some powerful way for where I've arrived in this moment. I seem to have come the distance at this point, and while there is more I could surely add to my story, I need to find us a finishing flourish. I trust Hippocrates won't mind if I borrow from him a modest handful of words I find exceptionally meaningful.

Vita brevis, ars longa.

INDEX

Z

www.ingramcontent.com/pod-product-compliance
Lightning Source LLC
Chambersburg PA
CBHW020439290526

45785CB00002B/930